William Cochrane

The heavenly vision : and other sermons (1863-73)

William Cochrane

The heavenly vision : and other sermons (1863-73)

ISBN/EAN: 9783337085964

Printed in Europe, USA, Canada, Australia, Japan

Cover: Foto ©Lupo / pixelio.de

More available books at **www.hansebooks.com**

THE
HEAVENLY VISION;

AND OTHER SERMONS.

(1863-73

BY THE
REV. WILLIAM COCHRANE, M.A.
(Zion Presbyterian Church, Brantford.)

TORONTO:
ADAM, STEVENSON & CO.
1874.

Entered according to the Act of the Parliament of Canada, in the year one thousand eight hundred and seventy-four, by The Reverend William Cochrane, in the office of the Minister of Agriculture.

W. G. GIBSON, PRINTER,
KING STREET EAST, TORONTO.

TO THE

OFFICE-BEARERS AND CONGREGATION

OF

Zion Presbyterian Church

BRANTFORD

*Whose fond attachment and kind forbearance have lightened labor
and rendered sacred the tie between Pastor and People*

These Pages

ARE AFFECTIONATELY DEDICATED BY THEIR

FRIEND AND FELLOW-SERVANT

IN THE LORD

WILLIAM COCHRANE.

PREFACE.

AT the urgent request of members of my congregation, to whom the Sermons contained in this volume were first preached, I have consented to their publication. In making a selection out of a ten years' ministry, it is difficult to decide what subjects, under God's blessing, may be the most acceptable and profitable to the general reader. A minister is not always the best judge of the Sermons most calculated to do good, and is frequently mistaken as to results. The efforts that have been most carefully elaborated, are found in many cases far less effective than the spontaneous outbursts of the heart, under the guidance of the Holy Spirit. I have, therefore, selected the following pages without any special rule, and out of the ordinary weekly preparations for the pulpit, trusting that to my own people they may prove of some value, if not for their intrinsic merits,

Preface.

at least as a memento of happy seasons spent together in the House of God. Should the volume fall into the hands of others beyond the limits of my own congregation, and prove in any case a source of comfort and encouragement to God's own children, its publication will not be in vain.

BRANTFORD, April, 1874.

CONTENTS.

	PAGE
Preface	v

I.
THE HEAVENLY VISION.
"Thou shalt see my back parts, but my face shall not be seen."—EXODUS xxxiii. 23.
"They shall see His face."—REV. xxii. 4 . - . . . 1

II.
FEARING WHEN ENTERING THE CLOUD.
"And they feared as they entered the Cloud."—LUKE ix. 34. 22

III.
THE SOUL'S REST.
"Return unto thy rest, O my soul, for the Lord hath dealt bountifully with thee."—PSALM cxvi. 7 . . . 49

IV.
THE NUMBERER OF THE STARS.
"He healeth the broken in heart, and bindeth up their wounds. He telleth the number of the stars; He calleth them all by their names."—PSALM cxlvii. 3. 4. 77

V.

Things New and Old.

"Then said He unto them, Therefore every scribe which is instructed unto the Kingdom of Heaven is like unto a man that is an householder, which bringeth forth out of his treasure things new and old."—Matt. xiii. 52 90

VI.

Palm Tree Christians.

"The righteous shall flourish like the palm tree."—Psalm xcii. 12 113

VII.

An Immortality to be Desired.

"The righteous shall be in everlasting remembrance."—Psalm cxii. 6 137

VIII.

A New Year's Greeting.

"Beloved, I wish above all things that thou mayest prosper and be in health, even as thy soul prospereth."—3rd Epistle of John, 2 152

IX.

The Master's Call.

"The Master is come, and calleth for thee."—John xi. 28 173

X.

Touching His Garment.

"She came behind and touched His garment."—Mark v. 27 194

XI.

How Old art Thou?

"And Jacob said unto Pharaoh, The days of the years of my pilgrimage are an hundred and thirty years; few and evil have the days of the years of my life been, and have not attained unto the days of the years of the life of my fathers in the days of their pilgrimage."—Gen. xlvii. 9 217

XII.

The Builder and the Glory.

"Even He shall build the Temple of the Lord, and He shall bear the glory."—Zechariah vi. 13 234

XIII.

The Renewal of the Inner Man.

"Though our outward man perish, yet the inward man is renewed day by day."—2nd Cor. iv. 16 254

XIV.

Children in the Market-Place.

"But whereunto shall I liken this generation? It is like unto children sitting in the markets, and calling unto their fellows, and saying, We have piped unto you and ye have not danced; we have mourned unto you and ye have not lamented."—Matt. xi. 16, 17 . 270

XV.

THE BLESSEDNESS OF THE GODLY MAN.

PAGE

"He shall dwell on high; his place of defence shall be the munitions of rocks; bread shall be given him, his waters shall be sure."—ISAIAH xxxiii. 16 . . . 294

XVI.

AS A WEANED CHILD.

"My soul is even as a weaned child."—PSALM cxxxi. 2. 315

XVII.

THE ESSENTIALS OF PROFITABLE WORSHIP.

"Where two or three are gathered together in my name, there am I in the midst of them."—MATT. xviii. 20. 342

The Heavenly Vision.

"Thou shalt see my back parts, but my face shall not be seen."—EXODUS xxxiii. 23.

"They shall see His face."—REVELATION xxii. 4.

Moses has been upon the Mount with God. From His hands he has received the two tables of stone, whereon was written the Law by the finger of God. Finding that the people in his absence had cast off their allegiance to Jehovah, and made and worshipped a golden calf, Moses, in the exercise of righteous indignation, casts the tables of stone out of his hands, and breaks them beneath the Mount. Unwilling at the first to assume the leadership of the Israelites, such shameful apostasy on their part would, but for Divine interposition, have led to his entire abandonment of the work. The fearful crime having been signally and terribly avenged, by the slaughter of three thousand men, and the people consecrated anew to the service of God, Moses is commanded to resume the march through the wilderness. "Now go, lead the people unto the place of which I have spoken unto thee.

Behold, mine angel shall go before thee." Moses at once proceeds to execute the Divine command. The tabernacle is pitched without the camp, and as Moses enters, the cloudy pillar descends, overshadowing the door of the tabernacle, while the Lord talks with Moses face to face, as a man speaketh with a friend. Such signal favour and condescension on the part of Jehovah to his servant, emboldens Moses to seek still further manifestations of Divine power and guidance. He is for the second time to begin the journey, and just as at the outset, when he received his commission from out the burning bush, so now he desires a similar token of the Almighty's favour. "Now therefore, if I have found grace in Thy sight, show me now the way that I may know Thee." "My presence shall go with thee," God replies, "and I will give thee rest." Still, as if unsatisfied with the assurance of God's presence, he cries out "Lord, I beseech Thee, show me Thy glory."

Moses already, it must be borne in mind, more than almost any other Old Testament Saint, had been signally distinguished by previous displays of

God's glory In the burning bush he had listened to the voice of the great I Am. In that long series of miracles wrought against Pharoah and the Egyptians, culminating in the passage of the destroying angel over the land, and the death of the firstborn;—in the parting of the Red Sea, and the drowning of the pursuing columns of Egypt's mighty warriors;—in the pillar of fire and cloud that guided and guarded the Israelites on their way, —and amid the thunders and lightnings of Mount Sinai, the might and majesty of Jehovah had been strikingly revealed. Nor must we forget that for forty days and forty nights Moses was alone on the Mount with God, during which time the external appearance of God's glory upon the mountain's summit was like devouring fire, in the sight of the congregation. During that time Moses doubtless was a spectator of many things that mortal eye had never seen, and human reason can never understand. But these sublime manifestations only increased his eagerness to draw nearer, and nearer still, to the source of all true blessedness. The deeper he drank the more he thirsted—the more frequent his communion with his Maker the more earnestly did he long after constant intercourse. Thus it was that what in other circumstances might have seemed presumptuous daring, must be regarded as the cry of victorious faith, as Moses on the Mount of Transfiguration cries out, "I beseech Thee, show me Thy glory."

What is this glory of God? do you ask me. Just the character of God—the outshining of God—that radiant holiness which encircles the Divine attributes; —a glory higher, purer, and more solemnizing than that external glory which shines upon the face of nature. Such was the glory that Moses desired to look upon with unclouded vision. Nay, inasmuch as his request was not fully granted, it would almost seem as if, in that hour of ecstacy, Moses would have penetrated the unfathomable depths of the Divine Being, which are shrouded from mortal eye. It was evidently something more than what we are accustomed to call the declarative glory of God that Moses desired to look upon. He wanted not simply to know God, in the sense of having palpable evidence of His existence, but to understand in some measure what He is;—to have, in that secret favored hour when the world was shut out, and Heaven seemed so near, a manifestation of those perfections, which to the eye of sense are dark and lowering, but to the child of God are full of hope—of peace—of comfort—and holy joy!

Jehovah was evidently not displeased with the desire of His servant, though his prayer was not fully answered. Flesh and blood could not endure a direct vision of the unveiled splendour of the Godhead. The essence of God is eternally secret. When Daniel only saw an angel, he fell into a deep sleep; and John, at the sight of Him upon whose bosom he had often leaned, fell at His feet as dead. And therefore, in mercy to His feeble servant, God replies, "Thou canst not see my face and live, for there·shall no man see me and live." But in order to confirm and strengthen his servant, and as far as possible meet this strong desire of his heart, a revelation was made of the invisible God, adapted to the feebleness of the creature. "Behold," said God, "there is a place by me, and thou shalt stand upon a rock: and it shall come to pass, while my glory passeth by, that I will put thee in a clift of the rock, and will cover thee with my hand while I pass by; and I will take away mine hand, and thou shalt see my back parts: but my face shall not be seen." Hidden thus within a clift of the rock, and covered with the hand of Jehovah, Moses was able to catch a glimpse of the retiring Divinity, but the full vision was reserved, until his disembodied spirit should enter the upper sanctuary.

Fifteen centuries after the event recorded in these verses, on another mountain-top, Moses beheld the Son of Man, His face shining as the sun, and His raiment white and glistening. He had now enjoyed the beatific vision, and appeared clothed in the garments of immortality, holding solemn yet friendly intercourse with the incarnate God. For the moment the curtain that hides the invisible world from human gaze is turned aside, and we catch a passing glimpse of the inconceivable, inexpressible happiness of the saints in light. It is not now a shadowy passing view of the Deity they enjoy, but face to face recognition. They are before the Throne—they sing the song of Moses the servant of God, and the song of the Lamb. Humanity redeemed, glorified, and exalted, now looks with faultless vision upon the face of God. "They see His face, and His name is on their forehead."

In view of the statements contained in these passages, we remark:

I. That imperfect knowledge of God's perfections and works is a condition of our present existence. All that we can see is but "the back parts of the Almighty—His face cannot be seen." To the same purport are such statements of Scripture: "Clouds and darkness are round about Him;" "Canst thou by searching find out God? Canst thou find out the Almighty to perfection?" "Now we see through a glass darkly—then face to face; now I know in part, but then shall I know even as I am known."

It is not to be denied that great advances have been made in every department of knowledge in recent years. The world of matter and of mind have each in turn been invaded, investigated and scrutinized. Theology has been systematized, and advanced beyond any former age. The learned speculations of a bygone antiquity have become the pastimes of the present, and the profoundest discoveries of past ages are now regarded as hardly worthy of serious consideration. Turn the eye where you will—scan the universe of matter—penetrate the depths of mind—traverse the boundary line that separates the seen from the unseen world, and there we behold the daring speculations of the human soul. We send the electric spark of fire from continent to continent along the bed of ocean, and hold converse with the stars! Thus, in the study and application of those stupendous laws that continue our globe in existence, we see the face of God. The earth we tread and the air we breathe,—the universe and the conscience,—"the starry heavens above and the moral law within, are all so many witnesses of His presence and His power."

But yet, after all that has been discovered, how little do we know of God's mysterious workings in the natural or spiritual world! Nature throws but little light upon the higher perfections of the Godhead as they relate to mortals, and the most satisfactory discussions as to the method of God's moral government of His fallen creatures, leave the profoundest questions of existence unsolved. In the face of nature, and apart from revelation, many of God's attributes may be discovered. Yet, taken as a whole, Nature gives forth an uncertain sound. No true idea—no complete, harmonious view, of God's perfections can ever thus be obtained. It is not always spring-time and summer, beauty and sunshine; there is autumn with its falling leaves, and winter with its storms and tempests. The gentle breezes of the zephyr and noiselessly descending dew-drops have their counterparts in the thunder-peal and lightning-flash. What mean these volcanic eruptions, ceaselessly pouring forth their liquid fire, and encrusting whole towns and villages in their deathly grasp?—those frequently recurring inundations, where the avalanche of waters overflows the banks of rivers, carrying desolation in its onward sweep?—those earthquakes and tornadoes, which change the relative position of land and water, and hurl into confusion the very foundations of the earth? In such phenomena we see but "the back parts of the Almighty—His face cannot be seen." In Providence, again, how much there is to astonish and astound! The seemingly partial distribution of rewards and punishments—the many afflictions of the righteous and apparently uninterrupted prosperity of the wicked—the young and hopeful called away in the beginning of existence—

false systems of religion and degrading despotisms suffered to enslave the human mind and retard the long predicted reign of peace and goodwill, when Messiah shall see of the travail of His soul and be satisfied! And finally, in regard to the great doctrines that centre around the Cross of Christ, is it not equally true that we see but "the back parts of the Almighty?" How dim and indistinct our view of eternal realities—how perplexed and confounded are the noblest intellects of earth before the simplest truths of Scripture? In regard to Divine things— those secret things which belong to God—our knowledge is but rudimentary compared with the clear and full revelation that shall be enjoyed hereafter. There is an almost infinite distance between the highest gifts and noblest attainments of earth, and the unbounded and accurate perceptions of the saints in heaven. This world is, after all, but the cradle of the human intellect, and the profoundest thinkers are but babes. "What we see of God here is but a broken reflection, infinitely less like God than the sparkle of the morning dew-drop is like the glorious sun of heaven." All that Moses saw, or that any of us see, of God on earth, is but "a gleam of day, let into the chinks of the soul's dark cottage," and yet such visions form the most delightful moments of our life. Standing amid these but half revealed truths, which the angels desire to look into, and anticipating the moment of perfect vision, we cry out with the poet—

> "Oh the hour when this material
> Shall have vanished like a cloud,
> When amid the wide ethereal,
> All the invisible shall crowd—
> And the naked soul, surrounded
> With innumerous hosts of light,
> Triumph in the view unbounded,
> And adore the Infinite."

For, though it is only "the back parts of the Almighty" that we see, we have in them promise of better days to come. There could be no shadow unless there were something real to cast the shadow. Our present imperfect knowledge of Divine things is the earnest of a higher condition of existence, when every inquiry of the human soul shall be fully satisfied. If we do not always behold the sun, the shining of the moon, which reflects the light of the greater orb, is evidence of its existence. So, in like manner, the glimpses of truth which we now possess are but faint reflections of that Sun of Righteousness in whose light we shall see light clearly. There is something, then, for faith to rest upon. The world beyond is not a mere phantasy. Our instincts and intuitions, seeking and searching after an existence higher and nobler than the present, are not the dreams of a disordered mind. They stimulate to nobler efforts and holier lives; for every man that hath the hope of seeing God, purifies himself, even as Christ is pure.

And this brings me to notice:

II. That in our future state of existence our knowledge of God shall be more satisfactory;—His perfections and works, in providence and grace, shall be more fully revealed and more perfectly understood—" We shall see His face."

Can it be possible for such worms as we are to see God? Yes, most assuredly. Says the Psalmist: "As for me, I shall behold Thy face in righteousness; I shall be satisfied when I awake with Thy likeness." Says Job: "I know that my Redeemer liveth, and that He shall stand at the latter day upon the earth. And though after my skin, worms destroy this body, yet in my flesh shall I see God: Whom I shall see for myself, and mine eyes shall behold ånd not another." "Blessed are the pure in heart," says Christ, "for they shall see God;" and to the same purport are the words of Paul and John. "We all, with open face beholding as in a glass the glory of the Lord, are changed into the same image from glory to glory." "Beloved, now are we the sons of God, and it doth not yet appear what we shall be; but we know that, when He shall appear, we shall be like Him, for we shall see Him as He is."

It is not well to dogmatize respecting the enjoyments and privileges of the saints in heaven. It is in bold outlines, not in minute details, that the future state of existence is painted on the canvas. We see, as it were, but the headlands, and more prominent outstanding objects that lie within the eternal world, just as Moses from Mount Nebo saw the widespread panorama of the Promised Land beyond the swellings of the Jordan. Much is left for a sanctified faith to fill in and complete. And is it not well that it is so ordered? No human soul could bear clearer visions of heaven's undimmed glory than faith supplies. Even now, when we soar to the external heavens, and endeavour by the exercise of intellect to grasp those suns and systems that skirt the boundaries of immensity, we feel oppressed and wearied in our feeble efforts. If so while attempting to survey the outer carpet of the spirit world, what would it be were we admitted to the Holy of Holies—to walk those golden streets and hear the songs of the angelic choir!

And yet such passages as our text, and others referred to, are clearly intended to teach us something of the state beyond the grave. While we may not presume to be wise above what is written, it is our privilege to know the mind of the Spirit. How the glorified are to see God,—the full extent and nature of that vision,—we may not describe. This much we know, that we shall recognize the Saviour—that He shall be the central object of attraction to the inhabitants of that blessed state—without whose presence Heaven would be shorn of all its happiness. And may we not advance one step further, and believe that the sight and presence of God in Heaven implies communion with Him—the interchange of thought, fellowship and friendship, better far than that which even Moses enjoyed upon the Mount? Are the privileges of God's children in the glorified state to be less than that of the visitors on the Mount of Transfiguration, who talked with one another and with Christ?* Are we simply to look upon the glorified humanity of the risen Redeemer, and be changed into His image, as we would look with admiring wonder on some faultless specimen of art? Or is it not rather implied that our friendship and fellowship shall be of the most endearing character, far transcending the highest forms of saintly experience on earth; that those same burning tones of love that arrested Mary in the

---

* "If the contemplation of Christ's glorified manhood so filled the Apostle with joy that he was unwilling to be sundered from it, how shall it fare with those who attain to the contemplation of his glorious Godhead? And if it was so good a thing to dwell with two of His saints, how then to come to the heavenly Jerusalem, to the general assembly and Church of the first-born that are written in heaven, and to God the Judge of all—these not seen through a glass darkly, but face to face?"—*Anselm*.

garden, when He called her by name, and made her conscious that she stood in the presence of her risen Lord, shall bring us also near to Him, "as we hear from His own lips the story of Nazareth and Bethany and Golgotha"—of the chilly mountains where He prayed for us, and the desert places where He hungered. Surely this much we may believe of Him who made the hearts of the disciples burn within them "as He talked to them by the way," and opened up to them the Scriptures.

Now, in view of such intimacy between the redeemed and the Redeemer, and under such teaching, who can set limits to the believer's attainments in the highest forms of spiritual knowledge? We shall then have more than mere guesses after truth;—speculation, and uncertainty, and surmises shall end, and clear and definite apprehensions of truth prevail. Doctrines and decrees, that have perplexed the human mind for ages, shall be resolved in the light of Heaven, and command the admiration of its highest intelligences. Mysteries shall then all be made plain,—secrets revealed, and dark dispensations flooded with light. "With Thee," says the

Psalmist, "is the fountain of light, and in Thy light shall we see light." "The city," says John, "has no need of the sun, neither of the moon to shine in it, for the glory of God lightens it, and the Lamb is the light thereof."

Thus to see God, demands and implies entire and final separation from sense and sin. It is by the regenerated and perfected soul that God is seen as He is. Now we see Him as we are. Our conception is formed from the poor materials we have in ourselves. But when this mortal puts on immortality, and this corruptible incorruption, our conception of the Infinite God shall be vastly different. In proportion to the sinlessness of our nature shall be our accurate apprehension of God's perfections, and therefore we are distinctly told that into that holy region "there shall in no wise enter in anything that defileth, but only those whose names are written in the Lamb's Book of Life;" and that, without holiness, no man can see God in peace. The simple fact that they are admitted to Heaven, and see His face, and are near the throne, and have Jehovah's name inscribed on their foreheads, is evidence of their acceptance. Their sins have all been pardoned on the grounds of Christ's atonement—they have been reconciled to an offended God through the intercession of the Saviour. They stand clothed in His righteousness, and arrayed in the garments of holiness. Heaven is a condition of heart, as well as a locality. Perfect purity of heart, full conformity to God's will, and unconstrained obedience to his behests, characterize all these children of God. For seeing God implies active service. "They serve Him day and night in His temple." The sight and the service are intimately connected in the text. It is not true that

> "All we know of saints above,
> Is that they sing, and that they love."

We know from Scripture, and we argue from the constitution of the human soul, that Heaven must be a place where the highest aspirations of the soul shall have their fullest development. "An instrument, wrought up at so much expense to a polished fitness for service, is surely never destined to be suspended on the palace walls of heaven." No! "Trained in a school, purified in a furnace—

loved with a love which the seraphim and cherubim have never known and never needed; instinct with yearnings and strivings after the high, the beautiful and immortal, we cannot doubt that the service of the Lord's redeemed, accompanied with the sight of his blessed countenance, will be yet higher and nobler than the services of the happy and glorious, but unfallen and unpurchased angels." To the saint of God the approach of death is but the call to higher service.

> "Go hence to yonder temple, filled with glory,
> There shalt thou praise thy Lord in song and story;
> There shalt thou see His face, instinct with beauty,
> There shalt thou serve with all delightsome duty."

Have you, my hearer, a hope of seeing God? Most men have. Saint and sinner alike shall see Him. "Behold he cometh with clouds, and every eye shall see Him, and they also which pierced Him." But in the one case, the sight shall produce feelings of despair, in view of a sentence compared with which annihilation were an envied punishment. "Fall on us and hide us from the face of Him that sitteth upon the throne, and from the wrath of the Lamb; for the great day of His wrath is

come and who shall be able to stand?" Such are
the words of the impenitent and unpardoned. The
sight of God in such circumstances means more
than a simple recognition of the terrible anger of
Almighty God;—more than hearing the sentence of
condemnation. It means that the sinner shall con-
cur in its justice while shrinking from its awful
consequences. For if the faculties of the redeemed
soul in its disembodied state, shall be enlarged and
clarified so as to possess a more accurate conception of God's love and tenderness, will not the
sinner also understand, as he has never understood
before, the fiery vengeance of the Lamb? May not
the torments of hell be largely made up of remorse
occasioned by the memory of past ingratitude, and
the ever increasing perception of God's wondrous
patience and forbearance towards the now eternally
abandoned sinner. If you would see God in other
and happier circumstances, as your friend and not
your foe, you must see Him now as your Saviour.
"Acquaint now thyself with Him and be at peace;
thereby good shall come unto thee. Kiss the Son,
lest He be angry and ye perish from the way
when His wrath is kindled but a little."

In sure prospect of "seeing God's face" His saints can patiently wait for fuller and more satisfactory disclosures of His perfections than are possible on earth. What we know not now we shall know hereafter. The broken and tangled threads of Providence shall yet be united and unravelled. The ways of God to man shall be fully vindicated. Meanwhile, let us reverently seek to know His will and follow the leadings of His spirit, though it be with faltering step—saying with the poet:

> "To Him, from wanderings long and wide
> I come, an overwearied child,
> Assured that all I know is best,
> And humbly trusting for the rest."

Fearing when Entering the Cloud.

"**And they feared as they entered the cloud.**"—LUKE, IX. 34.

The Transfiguration of Christ is one of the most remarkable events recorded in Scripture. After all the learning and study bestowed upon it by representative men of the different schools and churches, but comparatively little has been done to furnish a satisfactory solution of its many difficulties. Most probably it is one of those incidents the full meaning of which cannot be revealed to mortals; surrounded by mysteries which we cannot penetrate, and suggesting queries which we cannot answer.

It is not difficult, however, to conjecture at least, why the disciples named—as representing the entire brotherhood—were made spectators of such a scene. Before this, Christ had intimated more than once, and in no doubtful language, His approaching sufferings and death;—an announcement that never fell upon the ears of the disciples without causing them intense pain and depression of spirits. In some cases, indeed, they remained incredulous, and unconvinced of the sincerity and reality of His words, "the hour is near at hand." In their affection for the Master they could not bear the thought of His leaving them—least of all that He should die by crucifixion—even if His death were followed by a glorious resurrection and ascension to the right hand of God. But it was absolutely necessary that, in some way or other, they should be prepared for what was inevitable, and comforted in the prospect of a separation, though it should require some supernatural testimony to His divinity and supreme authority in earth and Heaven. For this end, accompanied by three of His disciples who were always near the Master on special occasions, Christ ascended the mountain—not Mount Tabor, as has generally been supposed without any good cause,—but Mount Hermon, or some such lofty, sequestered spot, where, alone amid the solitudes of Nature, He might hold fellowship with His Father, and unburden His soul of its human sorrows. This, in itself, was no strange act of the Saviour. All through His earthly existence we find Him seeking such seasons of rest from the rasping cares and exhausting labours of an intensely busy life. Amid the stillness of Nature He found an outlet for the profound and awful secrets of the mind, and in its silent sympathy and tenderness felt unspeakable relief. As He prayed, we are told that the fashion of His countenance was altered, and His raiment became white and glistening;—His face shone as the sun, and His raiment was white as the light—exceeding white as snow, so as no fuller's earth can white them. Without attempting to be wise above what is written, or to suggest philosophic reasons for this wonderful spectacle, we may safely presume that this light was from within, and not from without. It was no common brilliancy. Christ's face was like a beam of light—one dazzling blaze of glory—too much for mortal eye to gaze upon. The sceptical theory of Rationalists, that the radiance of an Eastern sunset gleamed around Him as He prayed, and gave an additional element to the glory that transfigured Him, may have an element of truth in it, but nothing more. Nor must we ascribe it to that high enthusiasm and strong emotion which at times change the countenance and indicate the presence of noble feelings within the mind. We all know that the human face is dependent for much of its expression upon the soul; that even the most unimpassioned and stolid features may, in times of extraordinary rapture and excitement, become glowing and radiant. But more than this is requisite to account for the appearance of the Saviour upon the Mount of Transfiguration. The Saviour had often before been seen by His disciples after seasons of communion with His Father, but never as He now stood before them. There was more than the mere passing glow of devotional feeling; it was indicative of a nearness to the Divine Being, and the enjoyment of a higher state of celestial communion than is conceivable by mortals; a condition exceptional even in Christ's earthly experience, and intended for some very special end.

And now, as He thus stands transfigured before the disciples, two eminent saints are seen standing and communing with Him, Moses and Elias—the one representing the Law, and the other the Prophets—and both together representing the Old Testament declarations of the Divinity of the Son of God. These glorified ones, like the Saviour, are clothed in celestial raiment, in keeping with the transcendent glory of the Messiah. Their conversation is of Divine things;—concerning the decease which Christ was soon to accomplish at Jerusalem —the very subject concerning which the disciples were both ignorant and sceptical, but which was essential for their own personal comfort, and the faithful discharge of their public labors when the Master had gone. Such a scene—the transfigured Saviour, and the celestial visitors, and such conversation—in any circumstances would have been startling and bewildering, but specially so when coming upon the disciples unexpectedly, and with their views so unsettled and unsatisfactory as regards the predicted departure of the Master. During the early stages of this sublime manifestation of the Deity, Peter and his companions were asleep, but awakening from their drowsiness ere the vision had passed away—like men from their dreams, by some alarming tokens of judgment—they were permitted to gaze upon the transfigured Saviour; a sight in the main reserved for the Heavenly world. Captivated, amazed, transfixed with the spectacle,

Peter gives vent to his deep emotion by saying "It is good to be here; let us make three tabernacles—one for Thee, one for Moses, and one for Elias." It was indeed good to be there at such a moment, although the proposal of Peter seemed more the offspring of impulse than of reason. He indeed knew not what he said. Like men stunned and overpowered—unable to describe their feelings—lifted up, for the time being, far beyond the limits of human existence, how could we expect the calm reasoning and mature reflections that befitted such a scene!

But the vision cannot tarry. The time has not yet come for the Saviour to assume a glorified exterior. Moses and Elias have fulfilled their part, and must return to their glorified dwelling, leaving the Saviour behind to suffer. And now a cloud—no common cloud that visits the heavens, but the Sheckinah cloud, the pavilion of the manifested presence of God with His people upon earth—overshadows this strange, unearthly group—a gathering made up of the Divine and the human—the earthly and the heavenly—the sensual and the spiritual.

It is a terrible moment to these disciples, as yet unprepared for immediate translation to the inner mount of the Heavenly world. Their spirits fail them. What shall be the issue they cannot tell. Possibly the remains of Jewish superstition still haunt their minds and disturb their simple trust in a present all-powerful and all-merciful Saviour. Need we wonder that "they feared as they entered into the cloud." But hark! a voice speaks from out the cloud: "This is My Son: hear Him,"—and now all is silent. The cloud vanishes, and with the vanishing of the overshadowing cloud Moses and Elias speed them upwards, beyond the confines of this lower world, to their eternal home; while the Saviour, touching the now prostrate, terror-stricken disciples, calms their fears by saying "Arise and be not afraid." Looking up, behold, Jesus is alone. The Transfiguration is ended—the disciples prepared for the coming departure, and assured of the coming victory of the Master, and strengthened inwardly for days of coming woe!

We cannot have such wonderful revelations of Christ, and the now glorified inhabitants of the upper world, as were given to Peter, James and John. But we may still enjoy very singular and striking displays of His power and glory. The object of such manifestations is to strengthen our faith—to inspire our hopes—and increase our desires after a higher and purer style of communion with Heaven than is common to the mass of Christians. It is only upon the mountain-top such scenes can possibly be witnessed; but many who make the mountain-top a frequent resort are never favoured with them. And when we are enveloped in the cloud—when, in answer to our cries and longings, we are hidden in the pavilion, how often are our feelings those of the disciples: "They feared when they entered into the cloud."

Let us look at this interesting thought for a little. First: It is not unnatural that in such circumstances we should fear, and for a time lose that spiritual consciousness which is necessary to profitable fellowship with the unseen. From the moment of man's fall in Eden, on to the present, the relations existing between the Creator and the creature have been entirely changed. Before that there was intimate communion between God and man, undisturbed by any elements of fear. There was, indeed, no cause for terror on the part of man, pure and innocent, in the presence of a holy God. But from the time that man wilfully disobeyed his Maker, and consciously brought down upon himself the threatened judgment of Heaven, those feelings of holy joy and calm delight, which were formerly his experience, have given place to far different emotions. The moment that the conscience of Adam was awakened to his sin, that moment he fled from the presence of his Maker, and vainly sought shelter from the searching eye of Omniscience amid the trees of the garden. And in spite of the reconciliation that has been effected by the death of Christ, enabling the child of God to come with trust and confidence to his Maker, we cannot altogether divest ourselves of those feelings and emotions. "Shall mortal man be more just than God? Shall a man be more pure than his Maker? Behold, He putteth no trust in his servants; and His angels He chargeth with folly. How much less in them that dwell in houses of clay, whose foundation is in the dust—which are crushed before the moth?"

Fearing when Entering the Cloud.

I am not now describing the feelings of ungodly men when venturing into the presence of their Maker, if such a thing is possible, but what is the experience of the best of God's saints. "Behold," said Abraham, when interceding for the Cities of the Plain, "I have taken upon me to speak unto the Lord, which am but dust and ashes. * * * Oh, let not the Lord be angry, and I will speak." When Moses, apparently ignorant that the Divine Being was present in the burning bush, would turn aside to see that strange sight, God called to him out of the midst of the bush, "Draw not nigh hither—put off thy shoes from off thy feet, for the place whereon thou standest is holy ground." The putting off the shoes was a confession of personal defilement, and indicated a sense of his awful unworthiness in the presence of the spotless majesty of the Divine Being. In the vision of Isaiah, when he saw the Lord sitting upon a throne high and lifted up—surrounded and surmounted with winged and flaming seraphims, who cried out "Holy, Holy, Holy is the Lord of Hosts: the whole earth is full of His glory,"—the same feelings of awe and terror possessed his mind. The posts of the door moved at the voice of the seraphims, and the house was filled with smoke, while the Prophet cried out, "Woe is me! for I am undone: because I am a man of unclean lips; for mine eyes have seen the King, the Lord of Hosts." And, not to weary you with illustrations of the point in question, need I refer you to the feelings of terror that possessed the apostle John in Patmos, when the glory of the Deity was revealed to his astonished vision, very much as in the Transfiguration to the disciples: "He heard a voice as of a great trumpet, and turning to see the voice that spake, he saw seven golden candlesticks, and, in the midst of the seven candlesticks, one like unto the Son of Man, clothed with a garment down to His feet, and girt about the paps with a golden girdle; His head and hairs were white as wool—as white as snow— His eyes as a flame of fire—His feet like unto fine brass, as if they burned in a furnace—and His voice as the sound of many waters; in His right hand were seven stars; out of His mouth went a sharp two-edged sword, and His countenance was as the sun shining in his strength." At such a sight, John tells us that he fell as one dead, until recalled to consciousness by the words "Fear not: I am the first and the last. I am He that liveth and was dead; and behold I am alive for evermore, Amen; and have the keys of hell and of death."

I know it is replied by some, that such feelings should never possess the child of God, who is assured of His Heavenly Father's love, and united to Him by a loving faith; and that, wherever they exist, there is evidence of unpardoned sin, and wrong ideas of God's relation to His accepted ones. I am not sure of this theory. I grant you that we entertain too frequently such views of God's character as lead us to crouch before His throne rather than lay hands boldly upon the altar, and that few of us exercise that freedom in the presence of our Maker, which is the privilege of His accepted ones. But that such emotions of fear, when we draw singularly near to the Shekinah, are evidence of unforgiven sin and conscious guilt, I deny. I find, in looking over the lives of the most eminent saints, under both dispensations, that just such fear was present when called into the immediate presence of God—a fear engendered not because of any doubt as to their acceptance, but increasing in proportion as they came nearer and nearer to the perfection of character demanded in the Word of God. One of the best evidences of progressive sanctification is a deeper consciousness of our own unworthiness and corruption, when seen in contrast with the infinite purity of the Divine Being; nor shall such holy fear be absent from our glorified state in heaven. It may not be the same unworthy, unreasonable dread, that now possesses the mind, but there shall be the existence of feelings in harmony with the infinite distance that must ever separate the saint from his Saviour—the Redeemer from the redeemed—the finite, though then immortal being, from Him who was, and is, and is to come, the eternal Jehovah, reigning and loving, through endless years. Surely if in heaven the pure intelligences that occupy that sinless place, and the elders around the throne, fall down before the Lamb, with their harps and golden vials, crying out, "Who shall not fear Thee, O Lord, and glorify Thy name, for Thou art holy,"—it will not be unbecoming for us, although redeemed and exalted, to

Fearing when Entering the Cloud. 35

fear, like the disciples upon the Mount, when we approach that great white cloud whereon sits the Son of God in awful majesty.

Secondly: We may expect clouds around about the Deity when favoured by such singular manifestations of His glory. It is always thus that He seems to reveal Himself to man. We cannot bear the direct vision of the Deity. "He is glorious in holiness—fearful in praises—ever doing wonders." When He would speak to man, or put forth such signal proofs of His presence and power, it is ever as when, in the destruction of the Egyptian host, He looked in the morning upon the host through the pillar of fire and cloud, and, troubling the enemies of Israel, buried them in the waters of the sea. I need hardly mention occasions when God appeared to His servants in clouds. When Moses was commanded to renew the journey to Canaan, after the fearful apostasy of the people, the cloudy pillar descended and stood over the door of the tabernacle, while within God and Moses talked together in familiar terms. When the congregation were assembled at the base of Mount Sinai to receive the law, there were thunders and lightnings, and a thick cloud upon the Mount, and the voice of the trumpet exceeding loud, so that all the people trembled throughout the camp. "Lo, I come unto thee," said God to Moses, "in a thick cloud, that the people may hear when I speak with thee, and believe thee for ever." When, on a subsequent occasion, seventy of the Elders of Israel were set apart to aid their leader in governing the people, "the Lord came down in a cloud" and took of His spirit and gave it to them, so that they prophesied and did not cease. And at the dedication of Solomon's temple, when the priests came out of the Holy place, the cloud so filled the house that they could not minister before the altar; the glory of the Lord filled the sanctuary, while the fire came down from heaven and consumed the burnt - offerings and sacrifices. And in the more private manifestations of His presence to individual saints, we find the same accompaniments. "I cried," says the Psalmist, "and He did hear my voice. * * .* The earth shook and trembled. * * * He bowed the heavens and came down, and darkness was under His feet; * * * He made darkness pavilions round about

Him; dark waters, and thick clouds of the skies. * * * Clouds and darkness are round about Him. * * * A fire goeth before Him, and burneth His enemies round about. * * * He maketh the clouds His chariot,—He walketh upon the wings of the wind." Through these clouds He looks down upon our world, and out of these clouds speaks to men. Say not then, in the language of infidelity, "Is not God in the height of the Heavens? And behold the height of the stars, how high they are! How doth God know? Can He judge through the dark cloud?" Ah! though thick clouds are a covering to Him, He seeth all, and walks in the circuit of the heavens!

It is so, still, that God speaks to His dependent creatures. And when, in Providence, He takes us into the cloud, how often, like the disciples, do we fear and tremble exceedingly! There is no man present, I venture to say, who has not at some time or other been called to enter the cloud, that seemed dark and lowering, full of dreadful calamities and overpowering judgment. I am not speaking of those clouds and gloomy shadows that men so often make for themselves,—mere figments of the imagination,—or contingent upon the condition of the body, operating indirectly upon the action of the mind. I am speaking of periods of mental and spiritual darkness that often envelope the believer, and are not in every case to be referred to or explained away by our unbelief and want of confidence in God. I believe that God takes the very best of His children into the clouds, not because their faith is weak, but comparatively strong; not to make them fearful, but courageous; not to punish, but ultimately to bless; not to let loose around them the tokens of His vengeance, in the thunder and lightning and whirlwind, but to refresh, comfort, and console, by secret teachings of His spirit that are impossible in the ordinary routine of a religious life.

> "When we in darkness walk,
> Nor feel the heavenly flame,
> Then is the time to trust our God,
> And rest upon His name."

Time would fail me to sketch, however imperfectly, such seasons in the history of God's people. There are clouds that pass over us, in the daily occupations of life, so dense and disheartening as almost to make us give up the conflict and weary for the end. On some few men the sun of prosperity shines without a moment's intermission. The world, to use a common expression, flows in upon them. They meet with no misfortunes or losses. Success seems to attend their every enterprise. Every year adds to their capital and their influence among their neighbors, and increases their social comforts. Others—better in character perhaps—seemingly as prudent, and industrious, and persevering, have to fight with insuperable obstacles at every step. They hardly know at times what is best to do. The future is dark and uncertain. They seem ever running against the tide, rather than with the current. The little acquired by strenuous self-denial vanishes in a day, and they are poor and penniless, like shipwrecked, dismantled vessels, abandoned and under a starless sky in mid-ocean, and left the sport of the fickle winds and waves. In such cases, if we believe that a good man's ways are ordered by the Lord and ordered aright, however different it seems to us, we must recognize a wise end in such periods of trial. We will value all the more highly coming years of prosperity, in proportion as we suffer adversity; the light will be all the more pleasant after having passed through the cloud. And then, need I speak of the clouds and sorrows of bereavement and sickness that darken so many Christian homes? When God emptied the cradle—when He took from you a husband or a wife—a brother or a sister; when death after death came into your home, and thinned the ranks of your acquaintances, and made you feel as if the rest of the grave were preferable to the continuance of life—Oh, how dark was that cloud—how dense! How lengthened its shadow over your heart and household! The darkened windows and weeds of mourning were but feeble exponents of the sorrow and grief that shrouded your soul, and the scalding tears that filled your eyes prevented a single glance upwards to God's throne. And yet, you must believe that the cloud was arranged by a loving Father, and its continuance ordained for some precious end; but the awful fear and terror you experienced during these days of loneliness can never pass from the memory. You "feared as you entered into the cloud." And finally, shall I speak of the clouds of scepticism—of perplexity—of doubt, and sometimes despair—that more or less trouble the minds of God's people, in relation to important doctrines of Scripture, and their own personal safety in Christ? Some know nothing of such "clouds," and cannot sympathize with those who are tortured by them; but their existence, and the misery they produce, are not the less certain. We say "how foolish to doubt! how displeasing to God! how unprofitable to question the love of God, and the facts of Scripture! how little we may understand of the one or the other!" And yet we cannot get away from these doubts. As one cloud is rolled away another darker and more portentous comes, robbing us of our peace, and suggesting the most terrible of thoughts. These are not the most faithless Christians who have doubts, or feel the most perplexed by fundamental truths. It is related of an eminent teacher that he used to call his scholars to him every evening, and ask them "What doubts had you to-day?" upon the principle that to doubt nothing is to understand nothing. "When a man comes to me and says 'I am quite happy,'" says John Newton, "I am not sorry to see him come again with some fears. I never knew a work stand well without a check!" It is so in every case of eminent gifts and graces; they are fostered and strengthened in the cloud, and not in the sunshine; and however much, like the disciples, we fear in entering into the cloud, the joy shall be more abundant when we emerge into the clear sunshine of Heaven.

It is such a state of mind that John Bunyan describes when Christian was called to grapple with Apollyon in the Valley of Humiliation. The combat lasted long—the darts flew thick as hail, while Christian became weaker and weaker. "I am void of fear in the matter," said Apollyon; "prepare thyself to die; for I swear by my infernal den, that thou shalt go no further: here will I spill thy soul." When called to pass through the Valley of the Shadow of Death—dark as pitch, full of demons and dragons of the pit—it was so terrible that Christian had almost resolved to go back, were it not that the danger of going back might be more than going forward. "But the day broke; the shadow of death was turned into morning, for God was with him, though in that dark and dismal state." And this leads me to remark:—

Thirdly: There is no cause for fear if Jesus is with us in the cloud. Nay, the very existence of the cloud is a proof, indirectly, that Christ is near at hand. There was nothing more cheering or assuring to the Israelites than the sight of the pillar of cloud. Equally with the pillar of fire it was the signal of God's guidance. When the cloud rested on the tabernacle the children of Israel rested, and when the cloud was taken up from the tabernacle they followed on to Canaan;—"Whether it was by day or by night that the cloud was taken up, they journeyed." There is such a thing as becoming so accustomed to darkness that fear is absent as much as in the daytime; and there is such a thing as tracing our way in the darkest of providences—Faith seeing and seizing hold of that hand which Sense cannot discern. There was really no cause for the disciples fearing as they entered the cloud. They were not alone. Moses was in the cloud, and Elias was in the cloud, but one better than these, Christ Himself, was there.

And so in all the cloudy and mysterious circumstances of life, let but the soul recognize and rest on Jesus, and there is no 'need for fear. "I will never leave thee, nor forsake thee," is surely a promise that covers every earthly condition, and is sufficient to allay every rising fear. After all, brethren, in the great majority of cases it is lack of trust and confidence in a constant Providence that causes fear, and keeps us oscillating so continually between joy and sorrow. Many of us exhibit far greater faith in the laws of Nature, as we call them, and the watchfulness of our earthly protectors, than we do in our Maker. Men have but little fear, in the dead of night, although rushing through the air with the speed of lightning in our modern railroads, when, humanly speaking, the safety of thousands is committed to conductor and engineer. And out on the ocean, when not a star sparkles in the sky, and the storm blows fiercely around the vessel, men sleep soundly and unconcerned as if on the solid earth, because they have unlimited confidence in the diligence of the mariners, and the skill and care of the commander. Why should it not be so, when called to make our way under the dark cloud of affliction and bereavement that God sends so often to curtain our sky, and hide from us the well known landmarks of existence? Nay, why should it not be so when we are called to enter the last dark cloud that interposes between us and the radiance of eternal day? Resting firmly upon Almighty love, we can see our covenant-keeping God in all the varied scenes of our earthly existence, and cheerfully follow His call.

> "He gives in gladsome homes to dwell,
> Or clothes in sorrow's shroud;
> His hand hath formed the light; His hand
> Hath formed the darkening cloud."

But there are others besides believers, who are called to pass into the cloud, and have great cause "to fear exceedingly." It is very true, as the wise men said, "that all things come alike to all,—one event to the righteous and to the wicked"—that, "as the good so is the sinner;" in other words that, in the present life, the righteous man may not seem more fortunate than his neighbor; but it is also true—invariably and literally—that the "fool walketh in darkness." In the case of the good man there is the assurance that in the cloud, and in the fiery furnace, there is One with him like unto the Son of Man. But in the case of the impenitent sinner, the clouds and darkness which may now occasionally encompass him are indications of coming storms, when the fury of the heavens shall burst forth upon his forsaken and despairing soul. For such my words of comfort have no meaning. I know not a more pitiable condition in life than that of a careless, unbelieving soul, out upon the dark ocean of existence, with no hand to guide his feeble bark, and no power sufficient to send a ray of light amid the darkness. Like some of these vessels that in recent storms have been cast upon the shore, or broken upon the rocks, becoming so unmanageable that no amount of skill or daring could prevent shipwreck—so are men who, in times of overwhelming providences, are cast upon their own resources, and left to buffet madly against the frowning billows of misfortune. In such cases they resemble the false priests of Baal, calling wildly for supernatural aid, without response. In bereavement there is no comfort for such men; deaths to such are judgments; the clouds and darkness that shadow their pathway are evidences that God has a controversy with them, and pursues them to the grave with relentless fury.

I have only time left to notice, without enlargement, two additional thoughts suggested by the passage. The one is, that often dark mysterious clouds follow extraordinary outshinings of the Divine glory. It was after the Transfiguration that the disciples entered the cloud; and, frequently, trials and troubles follow quickly signal tokens of God's mercy. The Valley of Humiliation is not far from the Mount of Exaltation ; seasons of darkness often succeed periods of unusual splendour. The morning of a bright summer day, the sun almost scorching the earth and drying up its juices, is often followed by a thunder-storm, when the heavens are lost to vision, and premature darkness ends the day. Both seasons are necessary for the earth, and both conditions are requisite for the child of God. And, finally, clouds are part of our earthly experience— in Heaven we shall see Christ without any intervening cloud. The day shall then break and the shadows flee away. We shall have no more cause for fear arising out of our sin. The morning star shall rise, precursor of our endless immortality:

> "When Time's stars have come and gone,
> And every mist of earth has flown,
> That better star shall rise
> On this world's clouded skies—
>   To shine forever.
> * * * Above our heads shall shine
>   A glorious firmament * * *
> A sky all glad, and pure, and bright,
> The Lamb once slain its perfect light;
> A star without a cloud,
> Whose light no mists enshroud—
>   Descending never."

Brethren, that time is nearer than we imagine. Are you prepared for it? When you think of that cloudless land can you say—

> "No shadows yonder!
> All light and song;
> Each day I wonder,
> And say, how long
> Shall time me sunder
> From that dear throng?"

The Soul's Rest.

"*Return unto thy rest, O my soul, for the Lord hath dealt bountifully with thee.*"—PSALM cxvi. 7.

One of the most profitable employments of the Christian is, from time to time, to hold converse with his own soul. However strange at first sight it may seem, it is not only a possible, but a highly beneficial exercise. Just in proportion as a man approximates his great original in purity of feeling and holiness of character, does he realize the existence of two entirely different elements in his mental constitution—the human, and the divine or spiritual. It is the province of the better part of our nature to give strength, comfort, and consolation to the weaker; to suggest grounds for gratitude and thankfulness in view of undeserved mercies bestowed, and thus to silence the uprisings of murmurings and rebellion so natural to the unrenewed man. Many a Christian almost on the brink of despair—full of darkness and melancholy—brooding over anticipated ills and expected adversities, has thus been roused to the higher and nobler duties of a religious life. It was so, times without number, with the Psalmist David. No experience is to be compared with his, in regard to its alternate seasons of joy and sorrow; helpless despondency, or strong, unswerving confidence in the faithfulness of his Maker. Now we hear the cry of the human soul,—sad, lonesome, and solitary, under the hidings of God's face;—and again, the outburst of praise from a heart reposing with amazing fearlessness in the presence of the Eternal. Take for example the 42nd and 43rd Psalms as an illustration of what we speak of; and as showing how a believer may comfort his soul in the presence of sudden and severe calamities. First there is the wail of a broken heart;—"As the hart panteth after the water-brooks, so panteth my soul after Thee, O God. My soul thirsteth for God, for the living God: when shall I come and appear before God? My tears have been my meat day and night, while they continually say unto me, Where is thy God?" And now comes the glad response of faith;—"Why art thou cast down, O my soul? and why art thou disquieted in me? Hope thou in God: for I shall yet praise Him for the help of His countenance." But again, we have the minor key, "O my God! my soul is cast down within me. * * * Deep calleth unto deep at the voice of Thy water spouts; all Thy waves and Thy billows are gone over me." Finally there is heard the victorious shout of triumph over all the suggestions of his weaker nature; "Why art thou cast down, O my soul, and why art thou disquieted within me? Hope in God: for I shall yet praise Him who is the help of my countenance and my God." Now such language, while it describes most truthfully and strikingly the feelings of the Psalmist under the influence of very different emotions, is also to be regarded as the exponent of the natural and spiritual man. We are not simply compound beings as regards matter and mind, but, when we arrive at a certain stage of our spiritual existence, there is a still further division of the mental part of our constitution;—the one being under the guidance and control of heavenly influences, and the other under subjection to the lower, or carnal impulses of earth. The apostle Paul recognized this fact in his own experience when he says: "I—that is the better portion of my nature—delight in the law of God after the inward man; but I see another law in my members, warring against the law of my mind and bringing me into captivity to the law of sin which is in my members." Now in such seasons as I am speaking of, when the weaker part of our nature yields overmuch to the power of trial and temptation, it is the part of our higher being to present such considerations as shall check the downward tendency of thought. Addressing our souls as if they were so many separate existences, we are to bid away all unnecessary fears; call up before their remembrance God's unfailing mercies and continued love, and say, in the language of adoring gratitude, "Return unto thy rest, O my soul, for the Lord hath dealt bountifully with thee."

Without waiting to speak of the circumstances in which the Psalm was composed, from which our text is taken, I remark—First: That the rest spoken of may be regarded as the repose and peace that the penitent sinner finds in Christ. Whatever were the feelings of the Psalmist when he penned these words, his former experience, as gathered from the context, was anything but joyful. The words used are descriptive of great bitterness of soul—of intense and protracted suffering—of such feelings as may be supposed to possess a guilty soul in the prospect of certain death and coming judgment. "The sorrows of death compassed me, and the pains of hell gat hold upon me: I found trouble and sorrow." Even to the Christian, who is assured of his hope in Christ and of his final salvation, it is in some respects a "fearful thing to die." To pass from things seen and temporal into the region of the unseen and eternal;—to pass through the dark valley of death's shadow and swim the troubled waters of the Jordan;—to stand before the scrutinizing gaze of the Omniscient Jehovah—even though He be at the same time a compassionate and merciful Saviour—is surely fitted to produce solemn awe in the heart of the best prepared Christian. But how much more so in the case of the unpardoned soul? When conscience arrays in blood-red characters the crimes of life; when the punishments of sin and the precursors of hell flash upon the mind; when the fact is at last realized that a death-bed is perhaps too late to cry for mercy and obtain the needed pardon, and consciousness is at last aroused to the inevitable doom that awaits the damned— Oh, how terrible is such a crisis! Well may it be described in the words of my text, "The sorrows of death compassed me, and the pains of hell gat' hold upon me."

The desperateness of the case is only equalled by the blessed enjoyment realized by those who find in Christ an all-sufficient Saviour—one not only able to carry the load of guilt, but to impart solid and lasting peace to the anxious soul. To such an one how sweet the rest spoken of in my text! Sweet to the toil-worn cottar is the eventide, when he lays down the implements of labour and homeward bends, to enjoy his simple fireside pleasures and the refreshing repose of balmy sleep. Sweet is the soldier's rocky bed, as, wrapped in his martial cloak, and guarded by the starry sentinels of heaven, he lays him down to snatch a brief hour's respite from the horrors of the battle-field and the roar of musketry. Sweet is the rest and quiet of home to the storm-tossed mariner who has fought for weary days with the tempest, and battled with the furies of the ocean; but sweeter far is the rest of the weary, anxious, sin-oppressed soul in the bosom of its God—"A rest calm and quiet as the sunlight amid the shrieks and tumults of a pillaged town—steady like the shining of the moon above a battle-field."

Sinner, this rest may be yours. It is your original heritage, though lost at the fall. Now you are a wanderer far from home—distracted by anxious cares and dark forebodings of coming wrath—the slave of tumultuous passions and unholy desires. But there are still yearnings,—longings,—upward aspirations in your nature withal. The very unrest and discord that prevails is an index and evidence of something better to be obtained—a sure pledge that the soul that seeks this rest in simple faith shall find it. Just "as the restless streams and brooks fret their mountain channels till they reach their proper depths in sea or river, and the waves of the sea itself, disturbed by the storm, heave and sway themselves to rest in their natural and common level again;—just as the thunderstorm is the voice of nature's unrest, as she seeks to regain the wonted repose of harmony and law;"—so is the restless uneasiness and feverish excitement of the sinner an evidence of coming peace. So long as the soul is not wholly hardened, and dead to all impressions— so long as there is felt these outreachings after spiritual rest, there is hope. Our very restlessness and misery are at once the tradition of a nobler and happier past, and the prophecy of a possible nobler and happier future.

> "The soul that's born of God
> Pants to view His glorious face,
> Upward tends to His abode,
> To rest in His embrace."

Secondly: The rest spoken of may be regarded as descriptive of the backsliding soul's return to its God. "Return unto thy rest, O my soul," indicates separation, withdrawal, absence, either more or less prolonged from the fountain-head of all spiritual delight. God never forsakes man until man forsakes his God. God's spirit, indeed, never forsakes the believer's soul. But there may be sad eclipses of the health-giving light of His countenance; sad obscurations of His glory; dark and lowering outbursts of what seems vengeance and wrath. These experiences are occasioned not by God's absence from the soul of the believer, but by some intervening obstacle that prevents faith from realizing His presence. Our world is periodically enveloped in darkness, not because the sun has refused to give his light and warmth, but because our earth has revolved on its axis so far as to render the sun for a time invisible. And just as a very small speck on the lens of the telescope, or a very minute defect in the scientific appliances used in scanning the heavens and measuring the stars, may destroy the highest hopes of the astronomer, so a very small sin may hide from our vision a present Deity. A very slight cause may suspend the telegraphic communications between the two hemispheres. The chain of electric fire must be maintained intact, else the depths of the ocean give forth no reply to man's questionings. And so, in like manner, Divine intercourse between man and God is only possible where there is singleness of eye to discover His presence, and a listening, ever ready ear to hear His voice.

I need not stop to enumerate the many sad departures from God of which believers are guilty. Your own consciousness attests the fact. I would rather call your attention to God's earnest solicitations and repeated calls after His backsliding children. It would almost seem as if the happiness of the Almighty was more intimately concerned in the reception of the penitent wanderers than the interests of the backsliding ones themselves. Just as the eastern shepherd goes forth over rugged mountains and dangerous bypaths in search of the lost sheep, does our Heavenly Father seek after His erring sons and daughters. Hear what He says: "Return, thou backsliding Israel, and I shall not cause mine anger to fall upon you. * * * Only acknowledge thine iniquity, that thou hast transgressed against the Lord thy God." "Return ye backsliding children, and I will heal your backslidings." "Return unto Me, and I will return unto you, saith the Lord of Hosts." "O Israel, return unto the Lord thy God, for thou hast fallen by thine iniquity. * * * I will heal their backslidings, I will love them freely." The return of the backsliding soul to its God never originates with itself. It is brought back by the tender cries of love, and the outstretched arms of the great Shepherd, to its resting-place. *Under such appeals* the heart softens and relents. Like the Prodigal in a foreign land, bereft of all the comforts and luxuries of home, so the soul, accustomed to the rich provisions of God's grace, hungers, after a time, for its native food. The pleasures, and the sinful delights of earth, are poor substitutes for the favour and friendship of Heaven. Bye and bye there arises within the soul the earnest, anxious sigh for home. "I will arise and go to my Father." "Behold we come unto Thee, for thou art the Lord our God." "Come, and let us return unto the Lord, for He hath torn, and He will heal us; He hath smitten, and He will bind us up." "Oh Lord our God, other lords beside Thee have had dominion over us; but by Thee only will we make mention of Thy name."

My text, then, is the language of a convicted backslider, who has felt the misery, the loneliness, and the horror of being away from Christ. Under these repeated entreaties, and by repeated strokes, by direct calls of the spirit, by the ministrations of the pulpit, by the broken bread and the poured-out wine of the sacramental table, which so touchingly proclaim the undying love of the crucified Saviour; by sad and sorrowful bereavements; by blasted hopes and blighted prospects; by the rebukes of conscience and the tender admonitions and affectionate overtures of a grieved but gracious Saviour, does God woo and win back the soul that has wandered from its home. "Bless the Lord, O my soul, and forget not all His benefits"—is then the expression of the grateful heart—"who forgiveth all thine inquities; who healeth all thy diseases, and redeemeth thy life from destruction; who crowneth thee with loving-kindness and tender mercies." "Return unto thy rest, O my soul, for the Lord hath dealt bountifully with thee." Once again at rest, the believer says to his soul:

> "Cease, my soul, thy strayings!
> Have they brought thee peace?
> Come, no more delayings,
> Cease, thy wanderings cease.
> These vanities, how vain!
> Wander not again.

> "Thou hast reached thy dwelling,
> Safe, sure anchorage,
> From the perilous swelling
> Of the tempest's rage.
> These vanities, how vain!
> Wander not again."

Thirdly: The rest spoken of may refer to that calm, spiritual enjoyment, which returns to the soul after a season of unusual and prolonged excitement. It is one of the sad evidences of our degenerate nature, and the disarrangement of our spiritual powers, that even God's people cannot sustain severe and arduous mental toil;—cannot wrestle or struggle with God at the mercy-seat, or at His banqueting table, without relaxing that concentration of soul necessary to profitable communion. But here upon earth there are seasons when the believer feels the need of a nearer approach into the presence of God than the regular exercises of the Sabbath and the family afford;—when a severe effort is made to arrive at a higher standard of holiness than he has yet attained; and when, like Paul, he "presses toward the mark, for the prize of the high calling of God in Christ Jesus." For example, a communion season is drawing near when you expect to sit at the Lord's table. Conscious of many sad failures in the performance of duty, and great weakness of faith, you give yourself up to the work of self-examination. You shut out the world. Your mental excitement, overpowering the necessities of the body, makes you loathe your very food. As the hour draws near, your emotions increase in power and sensibility, until they reach a point almost unbearable, so that in the act of communion you are so far uplifted from the earth, and indifferent to external circumstances, that, like Paul when caught up into Paradise, you can scarcely tell whether you are in the body or out of the body. Mind has for a time gained a decided mastery over matter—Heaven over earth, and Faith over Sense. Such a state of mind the Psalmist refers to in the sixty-third Psalm, when he says "My soul followeth *hard* after Thee." "*My heart is fixed*; I will sing and give praise." "As the hart panteth after the water - brooks, so panteth my soul after Thee, O God. My soul thirsteth for God, for the living God: when shall I come and appear before God?" These glowing, heated, burning experiences, necessary to the spiritual advancement of God's children, are nevertheless accompanied with great bodily and mental prostration. The brilliance of the revealed glory is too much for the eye of the soul. The little earthen vessel cannot contain the full outflow of the Divine munificence. The shadow of the beloved is very grateful, and His fruit sweet to the taste, but nevertheless the bride cries out: "Stay me with flagons, comfort me with apples, for I am sick of love." The sense of God's love is so overpowering that the soul staggers under it. Although it is but the reflected glory of the Eternal that we behold, it is too much for the tabernacle of clay. The existence of joy, alike with the agony of grief, compels withdrawal for a time into the secret chamber, where, alone, the believing soul may reflect upon past mercies, and pillow the weary head upon the loving breast of a sympathizing Friend.

I think that it is to such feelings that the language of the text primarily refers. The context describes the experience not of a recent convert who has just enjoyed the blessedness of salvation, but of one who has been the recipient of manifold tokens of Jehovah's favour. "Return unto thy rest, O my soul, for the Lord hath dealt *bountifully* with thee." The special mercies received have far exceeded expectation. The hungry soul has not only been satisfied, but filled to repletion. Answers to prayer have been given speedily, and favours granted that were not asked. Provision has been made for every want, and grace promised for every new emergency that may arise. With such feelings did the pious Israelites return to their tents, when, at the dedication of Solomon's temple, the glory of God filled the house. "They went unto their tents joyful and glad of heart, for all the goodness that the Lord had done for David His servant, and for Israel his people."

Fourthly: I would remark that the language of the text may be understood as descriptive of the inward peace and satisfaction that a doubt-distracted mind finds in a simple, child-like faith. Some men grasp the truth without hesitancy, and meet with no obstacles. Others, of strong intellectual grasp, have to fight their way against prejudices—against reason—against a natural pride of heart not easily overcome. All men are not sceptics by choice, for surely it is a miserable feeling that there is no such thing as truth in the world; that a man is drifting onward to a future all uncertain and unsettled. The Sceptic, if he would but honestly reveal the workings of his soul, would disclose an amount of mental torture only surpassed by the infinite anguish of the world of woe. Now suppose such an one is led in humble, simple faith, to accept the doctrines of the Bible—to subordinate human reason to the claims of inspiration, and to receive as eternal truth what is therein revealed concerning the past and future history of the soul, what a load of anxiety must be lifted from the spirit at such a moment! From the dark, spectral, shifting sand-banks of human speculation into the clear sunshine of revealed religion, is as great a change as from the poisonous miasma of the gloomy cavern to the health-giving, cheerful atmosphere of the mountain-top. Words, indeed, fail to describe the joy that must possess such a heart, and the grateful praise that finds expression on the lips. Well does it become the feverish, disquieted, and doubt-troubled mind to say, when assurance has been found, "Return unto thy rest, O my soul, for the Lord hath dealt bountifully with thee."

There is left but brief space to discuss the rest mentioned in the text. Let a few points suffice. I need scarcely remark that it is spiritual. Rest or repose thyself *in the Lord*, says the Psalmist. Seek not for that rest in the creature, or in created objects, which they possess not. You may for a time procure abnormal rest—a partial quiet and freedom from distressing fears—by administering opiates that dull the sensibilites and stupefy the mind, just as the drunkard finds in debauchery relief from self-inflicted miseries. But this is not health-giving rest. The fever will return again with increasing virulence, and the weariness with accompanying languor. The rest spoken of is God's gift, through His Son Jesus Christ, to His people. The same kind Providence that has provided sleep to recruit the energies of exhausted nature, has provided similar, though sweeter rest, for the jaded powers of man's immortal nature. Nay, the rest of the text may be most fully experienced even when he body is racked with pain, and when refreshing slumber is a stranger to the aching eyelids. Many an agonized and bed-ridden body has been found united to a calm and peaceful mind, serene as the depths of the ocean, or the stars as they sleep in their golden couches. So He gives His beloved *rest!* Rest from the conflict and confusion of the world; rest from mental toil and travail; from an accusing conscience; from a disturbed and frenzied imagination; and from all the fears of coming wrath which surround the couch of the guilty and unpardoned; a rest constant, uniform, eternal, and abiding as God Himself. What philosophy cannot furnish; what poetic genius has for ages vainly sighed for; what the high priests of false religions have for ages promised their deluded votaries as the greatest good—a sentimental visionary heaven of the greatest calm—"where the echo of the world's strife falls no more upon the ear, and happy spirits, emancipated from pain and sorrow, summer high in bliss upon the hills of God,"—this Christianity, and Christianity alone, provides, to meet the yearnings of the human soul. "The depth saith, 'It is not in me;' and the sea saith, 'it is not in me.' It cannot be gotten for gold, neither shall silver be weighed for the price thereof. It cannot be valued with the gold of Ophir, with the precious onyx, or the sapphire. The gold and the crystal cannot equal it, and the exchange of it shall not be for jewels of fine gold." To the question of England's great dramatist,

> "Canst thou not minister to a mind diseased?
> Pluck from the memory a rooted sorrow?
> Raze out the written trouble of the brain?"

reason gives no answer but the silent helplessness of despair. But Christ comes to the drooping soul and says "Come unto me, all ye that labour and are heavy laden, and I will give you rest; take My yoke upon you, and learn of Me, for I am meek and lowly in heart, and ye shall find rest for your souls." Only He who formed the human soul, and is conversant with all its varied anxieties and longings, can give satisfying repose. And need I add that this rest is a present boon. All the blood-bought privileges of the sons of God are present experiences, not excepting Heaven itself, which must be begun on earth. We who believe *now* enter upon rest. It is not a simple pledge or promise

The Soul's Rest.

in the future, but actual enjoyment in this life. The rest of the soul in God, while it may differ in degree, *is identical* with the rest which remains for the people of God in the Heavens; and unless we *now* understand something of its blessed calm, we cannot hope for its enternal joy hereafter. The promise is, "thy peace shall be as a river, and thy righteousness as the waves of the sea. * * * Thou wilt keep him in perfect peace, whose mind is stayed upon thee;"—until the rest of the tomb is at an end, and we shall be forever with the Lord. After all, our *rest* here is imperfect and incomplete, but soon we shall inhabit a land "where no hot breezes blow upon earth's fevered brow."

> "Calm as the ray of sun or star,
> Which storms assail in vain.
>
> "A few more storms shall beat
> On this wild rocky shore,
> And we shall be where tempests cease,
> And surges swell no more.
>
> "A few more Sabbaths here,
> Shall cheer us on our way,
> And we shall reach the endless rest,—
> The eternal Sabbath day."

The rest spoken of is not inactivity—a sleep or suspension of the mental powers—but healthy exercise. Whether, indeed, the mind is ever entirely at rest, even in hours of slumber, is a debated question with philosophers. But the spiritual rest at all events, of which we speak, consists largely in the consecration and surrender of every faculty and talent to the service of Christ. Idleness, to an active mind, is wearisome in the extreme; the *ennui* and listessness of those who "*kill*" time, as they say, by gaiety and fashion, is the most burdensome of all distempers. The labour that a man loves, whether it be the study of the professional man, or the physical toil of the artisan, is scarcely felt. The body does become exhausted, but not the mind. But for the weight of the weapons wherewith it works, as has been remarked, it might think, imagine, and love on forever. Galileo, in his study of the planets; Newton, in mastering the solar system; and, in later times, Hugh Miller, in searching amid the rocks and quarries of his native land for "Footprints of the Great Creator," were so charmed and captivated by their researches and triumphs, that labour, whether of mind or body, was actual enjoyment. Now, if the congeniality of one's daily toil can have such wonderful effect upon the mind, how refreshing and invigorating, instead of exhausting or wearying, must be *work for God*. For this very end it was created, and only in so far as one reaches it, can pure enjoyment be realized on earth. It is because, to a great extent, men are employed upon objects, and following after pursuits never intended to claim the attention or homage of the human soul, that they are so restless and so careworn. The bird unaccustomed to the confinement of the cage,—taken from the woods and fields where, with ten thousand songsters, it raised its melodious notes to heaven,—cannot feel at home, however dainty may be its fare and gorgeous its surroundings. And neither can the soul of man, when restricted to ignoble and earth-born pleasures. Give to it such employments as befit its immortal nature—in keeping with the dignity of its origin and the sublimity of its future history—occupations such as engage the angels and the redeemed, and weariness and fatigue will forever be unknown.

Such employment we cannot have on earth; but in bringing souls to Christ, in helping to elevate the fallen and degraded, in seeking after a higher standard of conduct and a closer fellowship with Heaven, we may enjoy this spiritual rest. No obstacles can discourage the earnest soul,—no opposition impede its progress. "To him who believes all things are all things possible." Life becomes all the sweeter as sacrifices are called for, and acts of self-denial demanded, until we are gradually prepared for the state of the glorified, where—sense and sin unknown, and corruption and mortality left behind—we shall pursue with increasing ardour the attractive studies of Eternity. "When holy thoughts and works become to our souls as devoid of effort as song to a bird, or incense to flowers;" when we can say like our Master, "My meat and drink is to do the will of my Heavenly Father," then we shall form part of that great congregation who surround the throne "resting neither day nor night," and serving Him day and night in His temple.

Finally, this *rest* consists in the harmonious working of all the powers and passions of the soul. "Self-conquest" is one of the noblest attainments, and is the possession only of the Christian. "Better is he that ruleth his spirit than he that taketh a city." When a man is converted he subjugates his will, his desires, and aspirations, to the appointments of heaven. By nature these are antagonistic to all that is good, but grace can and does mould them into conformity with the requirements of a holy life. The soul of the believer is not like the stagnant pool—with no outlet for its fetid waters, and no access to the sparkling streams that trickle down the mountain side—but rather like the ocean, which although from time to time in commotion, is restrained and limited by its divinely constructed barriers. A man may be most actively engaged from morning till night with the details of business, with the minutiæ of government, or the principles of science—meeting with much that is fitted to annoy and irritate in the prosecution of his calling, and yet maintain a composure and serenity, all unknown to weaker minds. There is perfect *rest* within, howèver much discord and disagreement there may be without. Like the scientific appliance known in mechanics by the name of the "governor," which equalizes the speed of the steam engine, and gives a uniformity otherwise impossible to its revolutions, so religion in the soul of man guides, directs, and controls all its movements in harmony with the glory of God and the welfare of its possessor. Instead of wayward, fretful, rebellious outbursts of temper and passion, there is begotten a gentleness, a meekness, a humility, an adjustment and self-restraint which is emphatically the "rest of God."

I feel, after all that has been said, how far we come short of our theme. But to the man who is at peace with his Maker I need not describe in what spiritual rest consists. He knows, by contrast as well as by actual experience, what it is. And yet how little do we realize of the still more perfect *rest* of heaven, where not a grief or sorrow shall dim the horizon of our joy, or mar our uninterrupted felicity. Our calmest moments and our brightest days on earth are "like rainbows braided on the wreaths of storm." But

> "There is blessedness that changeth not,
> A rest with God, a life that cannot die,
> A better portion, and a brighter lot,
> A name with Christ, a heritage on high."

The Soul's Rest.

> " Hope for the hopeless, for the weary rest
> More gentle than the still repose of even !
> Joy for the joyless, bliss for the unblest,
> Homes for the desolate, in yonder Heaven."

I have been speaking in an unknown tongue to some here. They are "weary;" but it is not so much because of an overdriven body as a sin-burdened soul. Nor do they realise any escape from life's warfare, until, in the words of Job, the grave shall receive its due, and the "weary be at rest." But oh! *is this " rest " final ?* Is it to be coveted by the man who has no hope of rest beyond the hour of Death, beyond the Resurrection, beyond the Judgment Day? Ah! if my Bible speaks truly, there is no *rest* for the wicked. The troubles and excitements of earth are but the precursors of unutterable torment. Very quiet and peaceful may be the place of sepulture — where flowers breathe fragrant perfumes, and murmuring streamlets sing their gentle requiems over the sleeping dust, and cypresses and willows shed their leaves upon the grassy grave. But, ah! much as all this befits the *dead in Christ*, it is out of place as regards the impenitent. " The rich man also died and was buried, and in hell he lifted up his eyes, being in torments." * * * "The smoke of their torment ascendeth up for ever and ever, and they have no rest day nor night." Would you escape all this, my unconverted hearer? Betake yourself now to Jesus. Bid adieu forever to the refuges of lies, the vain and deceptive joys of earth, the hollowness and emptiness of all created good. Are you not yet convinced of the utter hopelessness of all your own subterfuges and devices to satisfy the wants of a soul that shall exist commensurate with eternity? Or are you perfectly contented with this miserable drudgery which sin entails upon all its devotees? If you have indeed made election—free choice of this servitude and slavery, in preference to the liberty and independence which the Gospel offers, then be it so. But I cannot believe that any man can prefer continued unrest and mental agony through life, followed by unending despair, to the peace and pardon which is to be found in Christ.

The Numberer of the Stars, and the Healer of the Broken-Hearted.

---※---

"*He healeth the broken in heart, and bindeth up their wounds. He telleth the number of the stars; He calleth them by their names.*"—PSALM cxlvii. 3, 4.

In the account of creation contained in the Book of Genesis, we are told that God made two great lights—the greater light to rule the day and the lesser light to rule the night. Then it is added, "He made the stars." To the unassisted eye these twinkling stars seem small and insignificant, contrasted with the sun and moon, that flood our earth with light and beauty. And in order to counteract that feeling in the human mind, which refers to God's care and interest only the more grand and glorious objects in creation, the inspired penman would have us remember that in God's eye there is nothing which has sprung from His hands unworthy of His sustaining power. The smallest star, dimly recognizable by the telescope on the very verge of the horizon, is the product of Almighty power as much as the mightier orbs and planets that revolve in space. And in order still further to deepen our sense of God's omniscience and perfect knowledge of the host of Heaven, the Psalmist David says, "He telleth the number of the stars, He calleth them all by their names."

Another thought that rises simultaneously in the mind, on a survey of the heavenly bodies, is the vastness of creation and the comparative insignificance of this earth and man. The Psalmist, living in an age when astronomy had but begun her discoveries, was struck by this solemn thought: "When I consider the Heavens the work of Thy fingers, the moon and stars which Thou hast ordained, what is man that Thou art mindful of him, and the Son of Man that Thou visitest him?" Such language was not produced by any feeling of scepticism as to God's providential care over man, and His love for the human family, but when he looked upward to these stars—beheld their number and splendour, and thought of the vast army of worlds stretching into space—all moving harmoniously in their appointed orbits, and constituting part of the domain over which the Almighty maintains a constant government;—he felt how infinite must be the guardianship which embraces man within its sphere of exercise, and how unworthy man is to share in such regard of Heaven!

Such thoughts cannot but recur to many minds at the present day, when the knowledge of other worlds and planets has been so greatly enlarged, and their number so indefinitely increased. It need hardly be stated that the sun and moon and planets which circulate around the sun and constitute the solar system, are but a small portion of the Creator's handiwork. Beyond these are stars and systems of stars, not like our earth deriving light from the central sun, but shining in unborrowed splendour, and revolving round other suns equally grand and glorious as our own. To the naked eye, these appear but specks of light upon the brow of night, many of them at such a vast distance—hundreds of millions of miles—that even to the most powerful telescopes they remain but shining points, though in reality much larger than our earth, and it may be larger than our sun. Nor is this the end of our researches in the starry world. Beyond these myriads of telescopic stars, are patches of light which do not at first sight seem stars at all. Like the finest dust or sand of ocean's shore, they seem but a golden band of light encircling the extremities of space. But on further investigation, we find that these are separate stars, and central suns, around which whole planetary systems revolve. And when we still further reflect, that stars may have been created thousands of years since, *whose light has not yet reached us*, and that stars may have been extinguished thousands of years since, though still visible by their light which has not altogether died away; surely with the Psalmist we are forced to say, "O Lord, our Lord, how excellent is Thy name in all the earth, who has set Thy glory above the Heavens * * * What is man that Thou art mindful of him, or the Son of Man that Thou visitest him."

If once more, leaving the solid facts of astronomical discovery, we give play to our imagination, the paltry insignificance of this lower world will appear all the more conspicuous. That amid such a multiplicity of worlds we should receive so much attention is wonderful,—that God should so constantly provide for our welfare, and supply our wants, seems marvellous—still more so that His Son should die to redeem from sin and recover from ruin. Yet all this we can believe, on the supposition that this world, though smaller in size, is vastly more important than other worlds—"the summit and crown of God's material workmanship." But what if this world of ours be but one of an infinite number, the centres of animal and rational existence? What if these other worlds are peopled by intelligent creatures, possessed of reason and will? What if their inhabitants belong to a higher order of existence than man—pure and perfect as when first they came from their Creator's hands? Can we in such circumstances believe ourselves of so much importance that the Almighty should single us out for a special display of His long-suffering, and should make this little corner of the universe the theatre of such a glorious display of love. Again, with the

Psalmist, we are forced to say, "What is man that Thou art mindful of him?"

Overwhelmed by such speculations, which have for ages filled the mind of man, how full of sweet assurance do the words of the text fall upon the ear—"He healeth the broken in heart, and bindeth up their wounds—He telleth the number of the stars, and calleth them all by their names."

Consider then God's power and guardianship, as displayed *in the continued harmony and order of the heavenly host*. "He telleth the number of the stars, and calleth them all by their names." "Where wast thou," said the Almighty to Job, "when I laid the foundations of the earth? Declare, if thou hast understanding. Who hath laid the measures thereof, if thou knowest? Who hath stretched the line upon it? Whereupon are the foundations thereof fastened? Or who laid the corner-stone thereof, when the morning stars sang together, and all the sons of God chanted for joy." "Lift up your eyes on high," says the prophet Isaiah, "and behold who hath created these things, that bringeth out their host by number; He calleth them all by their names." It does not demand an extensive acquaintanceship with the science of astronomy to be filled with wonder and admiration at the power, the wisdom, and the goodness of God. None but an atheist can contemplate the majestic order of the heavenly bodies, and the wise adaptation of means to ends that reign throughout, without feeling impressed with a sense of the infinite knowledge that is everywhere evident. To reason as to the necessity of a Great First Cause and the continued exercise of Almighty care, seems madness. For granted, as the Philosopher tells us, that there are laws and combinations of laws, in virtue of which our earth and the other myriad stars and planets revolve, what are these laws but new evidence of a master mind, and a supreme directing power, that keeps watchful guard over the creatures of His hand? And what but a Divine mind could at first fashion and arrange the order of the universe, and continue its silent harmony unbroken to this hour!

"He telleth the number of the stars; He calleth them all by their names." His power was not expended at creation. His wisdom was not exhausted in the mere creation and arrangement of the heavenly bodies. Before a single atom of matter had been resolved into star and planet, its orbit was appointed and its circuit measured. As a general upon the battle-field marshals his battalions and directs their movements, so are the elements of unconscious matter in their Maker's hands. The sunbeam that shines upon the monarch's crown, and streams in upon the darkened chamber of the mourning widow, and the star that directs the pathway of the mariner over tempestuous waters, all alike receive their commission from His hands. In all these we see

> "The signature and stamp of power divine."
> * * * * *
> "Stars countless, each in its appointed place,
> Fast anchored in the deep abyss of space—
> These are Thy glorious works, Thou source of good,
> How dimly seen, how faintly understood!
> Absorbed in that immensity of space
> I stand abased, and yet aspire to Thee."

He that numbers the stars and calleth them all by their names, is also the healer of the broken-hearted. "He healeth the broken in heart, and bindeth up their wounds." God's character cannot be fully known in nature—not even in the sublime study of the starry hosts. These may declare His power, and wisdom, and majesty, but they are silent as regards His love, and tenderness, and consideration.

The vastness of creation does not prevent the most minute oversight on the part of the Almighty. This is what distinguishes the infinite Jehovah from man, whose knowledge is confined to the present moment. The greater the breadth of our survey in this world but increases our ignorance of details. Those who by reason of their genius lay hold of the deep things of nature, are, in proportion, unfitted for the common business of life. They cannot stoop to the level of common humanity; they dwell apart, occupying a different platform and moving in a different sphere. But with God it is far otherwise. Things great or little have no existence in his eyes. From His lofty standpoint all the events of life are on an equality. The formation of the dewdrop, and the opening blossom of the wayside flower, are His care, and engage the exercise of His wisdom as much as the grander events that convulse the world and shake its kingdoms!

His rational creation are objects of the most intense and constant interest. The splendours of immensity, the glory of His Throne, and the praises of angelic orders, neither absorb His attention nor cause forgetfulness of man. "What is man that Thou art mindful of him?" again we exclaim with the Psalmist. What is this world but an atom amid countless worlds, brighter and more magnificent? What is man that he should influence the thoughts and actions of the Almighty? What is this globe, which we regard as the centre of creation, but a speck in the eye of Heaven? For aught we can tell, man, with all his wondrous powers and faculties, may be the least in the scale of intelligent being! But notwithstanding all, the facts remain none the less true that God is mindful of this world, and that while He exercises a general providence over all His creatures, and supplies their wants, He regards man as a far nobler work than planets or sparkling stars, and visits him accordingly. For, after all that has been said concerning the glory of the heavens, what are stars, and suns, and systems in themselves—ignorant of their Creator and unconscious of their existence—as compared with man, endowed with intellect and allied to Divinity itself? What is matter in its grandest combinations compared with souls that shall live forever? Surely then we can believe that the very hairs of our head are all numbered; that God, who knows the fall of every sparrow, who feeds the fowls of the air, decks the lily of the field, and clothes the grass in its robe of green, has a much greater regard for man, endowed with reason and immortality.

Amid all the ranks and conditions of intelligent Creation, *those that are broken in heart are the special favorites of Heaven.* Hear this, ye suffering saints, who sigh and cry in the loneliness of despair. "Thus saith the High and Lofty One, that inhabiteth Eternity, whose name is Holy; I dwell in the High and Holy place, with him also that is of a contrite and humble spirit, to revive the hearts of the contrite ones." "He hath sent me to bind up the broken-hearted, to appoint unto them that mourn in Zion, to give unto them beauty for ashes, the oil of joy for mourning, the garment of praise for the spirit of heaviness." That there are broken hearts in the world all around us, is but the every day lesson of life. The record of burning tears that fall from blood-shot eyes—deep-drawn sighs and bleeding souls—constitutes a large chapter in the history of our fallen world. Some hearts are broken by oppression at the hands of their fellow-men; others, through misfortune and disappointment; others by the cruel slanders of wicked men. How many wives have broken hearts through the infidelity and cruel treatment of their husbands! How many fathers go down with sorrow to the grave because of the misconduct of beloved children! How many young hearts are crushed, at the very outset of life, through the crimes of parents—pining to the grave in homes of wretchedness and woe! And how many hearts are broken by mysterious providential calamities! Yon widowed wife, clad in weeds of mourning, tells of the sudden wreck of hopes and joys that now lie buried in the new-made grave, while the mother wrings her hands in agony and cries aloud in sorrow over the now empty cradle of her first-born child;—"Rachael weeping for her children, and will not be comforted, because they are not." Ah! how good for us that the scroll of lamentation and woe, which lies open to the eye of God, is hid from human vision.

Now, above all this tumult of human misery God sits enthroned—not an unmoved spectator, as represented by heathen fable, but a sympathising friend. He has a heart to feel, and comfort to bestow. He is known as the God of comfort and consolation. Our great High Priest can be touched with a feeling of our infirmities, for, having Himself suffered, He is able to succour and save to the uttermost His afflicted brethren. There is no grief of which He is not cognizant, and no heart history, however sad, with which He is not acquainted. "He healeth the broken in heart, and bindeth up their wounds."

> "Come, ye disconsolate, where'er ye languish,
>   Come, at the Mercy-Seat fervently kneel;
> Here bring your wounded hearts, here tell your anguish,
>   Earth has no sorrow that Heaven cannot heal.
>
> "Joy of the desolate, light of the straying,
>   Hope of the desolate, fadeless and pure;
> Here speaks the Comforter, in mercy saying,
>   Earth has no sorrow that Heaven cannot cure."

Things New and Old.

"Then said He unto them, Therefore every scribe which is instructed unto the Kingdom of Heaven is like unto a man that is an householder, which bringeth forth out of his treasure things new and old."—MATTHEW, xiii. 52.

The first preacher and teacher of Christianity was Jesus Christ. He combined in His own person the two-fold office of professor and evangelist. It was absolutely necessary, and at the same time most fitting that it should be so. As the author and founder of Christianity, thoroughly acquainted with all its doctrines and laws, and understanding how best to present them to the comprehension of the humblest intellect, and apply them to the human heart, He alone could successfully establish the new religion. Just as the inventor and designer of a new machine is best qualified to describe its intricate workings and manifold adaptations, so the author of a new system of morality, so radically different from Jewish or Pagan ethics, was the best adapted to unfold its beauty and maintain its superior claims and merits against all objectors.

How Christ preached, and *how* He taught the multitudes who waited either occasionally or statedly upon His ministry, we can in some measure understand from His published discussions and parables. *How he prepared the disciples* for the work of the apostleship, and what instructions He gave them as to the essential requisites of a successful ministry, is equally plainly stated on the page of inspiration, although more likely to escape our notice. To this topic we propose now to direct attention.

The disciples, with but stray exceptions, when called to be "fishers of men," were destitute of what may be called the preliminaries of learning or scholarship. I do not think they were at all behind or below the mass of their countrymen of the middle class of society, but certainly they were not above them either in worldly circumstances or refinement. Two methods of preparation were open, in order to qualify them for their work. The

Saviour *might have instantaneously*, by means *of a full and perfect inspiration, put them in possession of all necessary truth*, and fitted them oratorically to convey that truth impressively to others; or He might choose the more laborious course of training and teaching—line upon line, and precept upon precept—which we adopt at the present day in our academies and colleges, in preparing young men for professional walks in life. The one may be called the wholly Divine or supernatural—the other, the human or natural. Now it is worthy of remark that in fitting the early disciples to be Preachers of the Cross, He chose the latter method for the most part. *That they were inspired* is at once granted; that they were also furnished with the power of working miracles to attest the Divine character of the new religion and substantiate their heavenly commission, is also true, but these mighty adjuncts were rather called forth by *the special circumstances of the age* in which they lived, and the people to whom they preached, than forming part and parcel of their ministerial training. It was as scholars at the feet of Christ, as listeners and students, as His followers from house to house and place to place, gathering up under His directions the essentials of a successful ministry, that they were at last qualified to go forth and preach the Gospel to the world.

The first lessons also, it is to be observed, were *of the most elementary kind.* It was by parables, so simple in themselves that the Sabbath-school children of the present day can master the details. One by one he unfolded to them the mysteries of His kingdom, not by dry abstract reasoning, but by narrative and picture. Even with all this coming down, as it were, to the level of their apprehension, they were slow to understand him. They came to Him once and again to explain the hidden meaning of these parables which they could not grasp. After narrating the parable of the sower, he rebuked them on the dulness of their apprehension:— "Know ye not this parable? and how then will ye know all parables?" But they had a patient, because a loving teacher—one who compassionated their ignorance, and was ready to help them in their difficulties. Day after day He continued His instructions, accompanied with the most minute explanations, until eventually they became quicker in apprehending the spiritual truths which lay thinly concealed under metaphor and illustration. Having thus, by a variety of parables (see 13th chapter of Matthew's Gospel), endeavoured to set before them the rapid growth and results of His spiritual kingdom, He puts to them the question, as a teacher would put to his scholars,—" Have ye understood all these things?" and they replied, "Yea, Lord." They had now advanced a considerable way in their knowledge and comprehension of spiritual truths; they were approaching that standard of proficiency which Christ demanded of them before they went forth as ambassadors to their fellow-men. And in order that they might have the very highest conception of their office, and covet earnestly the best gifts, he adds:—" Every scribe which is instructed unto the Kingdom of Heaven, is like unto a man that is an householder, which bringeth out of his treasure things new and old."

Let us endeavor to understand the meaning of such language. I believe it contains the essentials, under God's blessing, of a successful ministry, whether in apostolic or modern times; and it is just because the pulpit, in many cases, fails to come up to what the Great Head of the Church demands, that it exercises so little power at the present day.

By the things new and old *may be meant* the message of grace as opposed to the law. Although specially and primarily set apart as preachers of Christianity, the apostles were not entirely to neglect all reference to the former dispensation, which confirms by its history and prophecy the events of the present. God's unchangeable and eternal truth *is one* under every dispensation, and the minister of Christ can never be wrong in connecting new thoughts with old images, and thus exhibiting the unity and harmony of God's will. The Jew was to be taught that in embracing the principles of the new religion he needed not to relinquish one jot or tittle of the Old Testament morality, while at the same time, *and side by side*, he was constantly to preach the grand doctrines of the Cross as the completion of God's revelation to fallen man. Though a very good interpretation of Christ's words, *more than this is intended*, it seems to me, in Christ's address to His disciples. While old truths were never to be lost sight of, they were from time to time to be presented in new forms. The accomplished teacher must not only bring forth from his treasury things old and dead, but things new and living, "the one along with the other; the new in the garb and in the light of the old, and the old in its fulfilment and development of the new." In other words, the minister of the Gospel must not only have his mind well plenished with old doctrines and historical details, but he must ever be making new observations, gathered from his own experience and the knowledge of the world. All the departments of science and philosophy—all the wonders of nature and art—all the treasures of the past and present, whether contained in the Bible or displayed in the vast store-house of Creation's wonders, or seen in the marvellous activities and enterprises of the human mind, are open for his study. He must be like a rich householder, who has his house full of goods, so that he is able not only to meet his own necessities, but the multifarious demands of others. Holding firmly by the doctrines of grace, as old as eternity itself, he must vary his mode of teaching them, so that all tastes and capacities and conditions of life may be profited and satisfied. He must address his hearers in such a way as to present old truths in new forms, so that, like the Apostle Paul, with a praiseworthy craftiness he may catch them with guile. Like a well-taught mechanic, who not simply knows the names of his tools but how to handle them, he must be *instructed*—intimately conversant with the things of the kingdom. His acquisitions of knowledge must become his own by virtue of experience, and out of that personal experience he is to bring forth "things new and old" to meet the wants of others. Our Lord plainly tells the disciples that He had not expended so much labour in teaching them, that they might simply be wise themselves, but that they might impart to others what He had thus communicated to them.

So far, then, we gather from our Lord's statement that He approved of none for the work of the ministry who were not thoroughly indoctrinated in the principles of the new religion. They were to hold a similar place in the primitive church that the scribe did in the synagogue. The name of scribe, it is true, was a by-word for the corruption they mingled with the truth. Professing to be the only authorized expounders of the law, like their co-religionists the Pharisees, "they made the word of God of none effect by their traditions." But the office of a scribe, if rightly exercised, was not only an honourable one, but also a necessary one. Then, as now, for the good of society and the spread of religion, men were set apart from the common cares and anxieties of business and manual toil, in order to study the words and works of God. They lived for the most part a hermit's life; they knew more of books than men; more of dead languages than the common conversation of the street; they had little knowledge of, and far less sympathy with, the lower classes of society. In these latter respects the disciples were by no means to imitate the ancient scribes. Their mode of training was essentially different, while their qualifications were to be proportionately superior. The disciples did not sit, like Saul of Tarsus, under such doctors of the law as Gamaliel; they were not expected to commit wholesale to memory the traditions or wise sayings of the fathers; they were not taught to regard the ministry as a priesthood altogether separate from society, and apart from "common things and common men." On the contrary, Christ taught them that the poorest of the poor and the greatest of sinners were to be their special charge; that their labour was to be chiefly expended upon the outcasts of respectable society, and those for whom no man cared. Such being their mission, a very different preparation was given them. Not from books, but from His lips, and in daily active contact with the masses of society they were subsequently to influence, did they receive the requisite knowledge and attainments their calling demanded. Heavenly truths, in the hands of Christ, took the form of proverb, parable, and narrative. He drew His lessons from every department of nature and every vocation in life. The sower sowing his seed—the fisherman casting his net into the sea—the merchant busy in his store—the jewel seeker in search of pearls and diamonds—the relations of master and servant in every day life—the laws of commerce between debtor and creditor—unjust stewards and unjust lawyers—marriages and wedding-feasts—the tares, the mustard seed, the leaven—the fig-tree—the lost sheep—the lost coin—such like objects and actual occurrences in nature and in life were the texts from which He expounded to them the mysteries of His kingdom. Nothing was beneath His notice, and nothing was to be beneath theirs. All these things were to be used in illustrating and enforcing higher truths; everywhere and from everything they were to gather the germs and seeds of expanding thoughts.

Now what, it may be asked, were the results of such training? Did it serve the end intended? Were the early apostles apt scholars and qualified teachers of Christianity? Did they catch the ear of the populace and awaken interest? Were they ever found unable to meet the arguments and subtle logic of sceptical Greeks or sanctimonious Pharisees? Was there ever *one solitary occasion* when Christianity might be ashamed of her defenders and apologists, as it is to be feared Christ is to-day with some who profess to be His heralds? *No, never!* They spake with a force and power—with an aptitude and burning earnestness that proved the sincerity of their convictions, and carried home the truth of God's words to the conscience of their hearers. As it was said of Christ, so it might be said of these early apostles,—"Never man spake like these men." Allowance must of course be made for those supernatural endowments which the Master conferred upon them at the first promulgation of Christianity, in virtue of which immense numbers, as on the day of Pentecost, were brought to a saving knowledge of the truth, but we must not give the credit of their wonderful success exclusively to those direct and heavenly baptisms, nor yet to the miracles which they wrought. If the amazing success of the apostles in the first age of the church was exclusively due to their supernatural endowments, then we can gather no lessons whatever as to the training of modern evangelists from the Word of God, and must rest contented with our present attainments, without striving after better things.

In view of the conversation referred to between Christ and His disciples, we proceed to lay down one or two propositions worthy the attention of ministers and congregations at the present day.

The old truths of God's word must never be lost sight of in our preaching or teaching. We must never give the smallest countenance to the idea of modern rationalists, that the world has grown so wise and so learned as to be altogether independent of those cardinal truths of Scripture without which the past history of our race is an inscrutable mystery. The fall of man from his high estate of holiness, the universal depravity and corruption of all human beings, the utter inability of the creature either to devise or accomplish a method of salvation, the justice of God in adjudging the violators of His law to eternal death, the eternal love of God the Father in the gift of Christ, the matchless love of Christ the Son in bearing our guilt, and dying to blot out our sins, the necessity of the continued application of the Holy Spirit in applying the work of redemption to our souls and fitting us for the enjoyment of heaven;—these and such truths must ever form a prominent part of pulpit discourse. Nay, should it be, as it must ever be in our present state, that we are unable to explain many mysteries connected with God's dealings with the world at large and individual sinners, we dare not abstain on that account from a public declaration of their eternal verity. For example, because we cannot satisfactorily explain to the comprehension of the hearer the doctrine of the Trinity, are we to ignore all reference to it, as having no value in the scheme of truth? Because we cannot grasp the great questions of Election and Predestination, God's foreknowledge and man's freewill, man's utter inability of himself to come to Christ, and at the same time his accountability and danger in refusing to come; because we cannot explain the conditions of a future day of judgment, the nature of the resurrection body, and the employments of the sanctified state beyond the grave, are we to pass over all such topics as unfit for the edification of the body of Christ? Such conduct would be as foolish as to refuse to investigate and study the ten thousand mysteries of nature which minister so much happiness to the enquiring mind. It is only by the continued study of such important scriptural doctrines that we can hope to make any advancement whatever towards their clearer comprehension, or be in any measure prepared for the fuller and more perfect revelation of eternity. The Protestant Reformers of the 15th and 16th centuries, while abolishing the unmeaning ceremonies and heresies which had gradually crept into the Christian Church, held fast to their doctrines, and saved the Church from the influx of many deadly heresies which at the present day corrupt the faith. They were not ashamed to dwell on "justification by faith" as the only source of the sinner's reconciliation with his God, however distasteful it might be to the carnal heart, and however much obloquy they might incur in denouncing human systems and human creeds. And by such a course they not only maintained the Church sound and pure, but they at the same time enjoyed precious seasons of revival and refreshing. Indeed gracious revivals of religion have always been experienced, when "the faith once delivered to the saints" has been preached in all its integrity and fulness.

But while not neglecting the old, we must not as ministers *forget to present the truths of Scripture in such new phases* as shall best adapt them to the age in which we live. We are specially addicted to idolatry of the old. Old traditions, old forms, old systems of philosophy, assert a kind of despotism over the human mind, and become invested with a superstitious reverence fatal to every kind of progress. Knowledge and extensive erudition—mere book attainments—a smattering of ancient lore—the contradictory opinions of commentators—the decrees of councils—the ability to refute certain heresies and uphold certain disputed points of criticism, are reckoned sufficient to constitute a man a preacher of the Gospel. There is thus begotten an idolatry of intellect—a worshipping of dogmas—which is altogether out of place in a successful minister. The ideas instilled into the minds of students, that an extensive acquaintance with dogmas and heresies is the great source of pulpit power, is carried with them into professional life. In almost every other sphere of society *but in the pulpit, men talk naturally*, and so as to be understood by all classes. But in the pulpit ministers seem, in many cases, to avoid common speech and common illustrations, and from year to year drawl out the same forms of doctrine, in antiquated and obsolete phrases, to congregations as listless and unedified as the sleepers in the grave. The result is seen in the detachment of numbers from the house of God, and the lessening influence of the Church upon the world.

In thus insisting that the pulpit of the present day must be more alive than it has been to the actual wants of men—that it become a help and a counsellor amid the difficulties and temptations of life, as well as our unfailing guide to the realities of eternity—we demand nothing more than what Christ demanded of the first preachers of Christianity. Why do we preach at all? To indoctrinate men in spiritual truth? All true—but the greater part of our modern congregations know the leading doctrines of the word of God almost as intelligently as does the preacher. They have been taught them from infancy at a mother's knee, in the Sabbath-school, and in the Bible class. What is wanted is not simply the bare reiteration of these doctrines, but the bringing of these docrines to bear upon the heart and life. Preaching is not an end, but a means. No minister is warranted in thinking that he has fulfilled his part when a certain amount of truth has been delivered to a congregation. In the preparation of that truth there should be an intelligent conception of the special wants of the hearers, so that there may be *immediate* effects. A knowledge of the habits, special temptations, and manifold hindrances to holy living should be sought after, that the preacher may not fire his balls at random, or spend his strength in vain. Thus did such men as Whitfield, and Wesley, and Jonathan Edwards preach. Under their preaching "men heard the judgment trump and saw the advancing heaven, and the day of doom began to mantle them with its shroud."

Some hearer may answer: In such a kind of preaching you do not follow apostolic rule. Did not Paul boast to the Corinthians that he preached *nothing* save "Jesus Christ and Him crucified?" Did he not say to the Galatians, "God forbid that I should glory *save in the Cross* of the Lord Jesus Christ?" It is hardly necessary, in reply, to remind the reader that in Paul's preaching and teaching there is no possible topic or human relationship, or calling in life, or individual sin, or flagrant evil, that is not referred to. He did preach Christ, but in preaching Christ and Him crucified, he adapted his matter and his arguments to the special wants of his various congregations. He preached Christ, not simply as crucified on Calvary, and lying in the tomb of Joseph, but as a living, powerful, and regenerating element in society. The doctrines and morality of scripture, according to Paul's teaching, were not only to be studied and admired, but embodied in the heart, and conscience, and life of every man. He sought immediate as well as remote results from his ministry; *results visible now*, as well as at the bar of God. It was not that "Christ and Him crucified" was his one never-varying theme, but that *from the Cross* of Christ, as from a starting point and centre, he drew those arguments and influences which were best adapted to mould the opinions, sanctify the affections, and rectify the conduct of man. To accomplish this the apostle adds: "I laid aside all human art and' rhetoric, that I might the more directly and pungently address the conscience and touch the hidden springs of action."

We plead for such a comprehensiveness in the modern pulpit, not only for the upbuilding of saints, but for the ingathering and retention of sinners. If you fetter the minister, and chain him down to a recapitulation of mere truisms from day to day; if you say, you must not touch the ethics of commerce or national sins or individual wickedness; if you insist that doctrines and dogmas—which in many cases are rendered more mysterious by their very discussion—are to be the constant subjects of pulpit discourse, you reduce the pulpit to a nonentity, subvert the ordinance of preaching, and make the servant of God the slave of custom, none the less odious because common in many parts of the land. The Puritans were noble men, perfect giants in theology, and possessed of intellects and souls that tower far above the average of ministers at the present day; but who is there, possessed in any degree with the power of adaptation, would attempt to read one of their three-hour homilies to an ordinary congregation? And if he did, what good results would follow? Yet these men in their day did noble service for our common faith, and have left behind a vast treasure-house of learning. Such a style of preaching was best suited to that age, just as it has been remarked, men then used bows and arrows, helmets, swords and spears, instead of iron-clads, Spencer rifles and Armstrong guns. The day has gone by for such primitive instruments of war, and such a prolonged and elaborate style of address. The destinies of nations and empires are now decided in a shorter time than formerly occupied armies in mustering on the field of battle. Men live quicker and die faster than of old, and need in religious teaching concentrated effort, special aim, and skilful marksmen. After all our pains, the bow will be drawn at a venture unless directed by the spirit of God.

If such a style of preaching is demanded at the present day, the younger ministers of the various evangelical churches should study more of the outside world, that they may know men's wants and sympathize with them in their struggles. In our land, it is true, the ranks of the ministry are chiefly recruited from the middle and working classes. It is a matter of regret that there is not a larger infusion of the sons of rich and influential

men. But from whatever source we receive our
supply of religious teachers, if they are to be efficient in the pulpit and valuable in society, they
must be brought directly in contact with the toiling
masses of our land. The sooner the idea is exploded
that ministers must keep themselves aloof from all
social enterprises, and all co-operative agencies
that have for their object the good of those beyond
the pale of the Christian Church, the better for
themselves and the cause of Christ. The charge is
made that ministers as a class look down upon the
working classes of the land, and that between them
and the non-professing world there is a bridgeless
gulf. I do not believe the charge to be well founded.
How to bring the extremes of society face to face,
and gather into our churches the sceptical and indifferent, is a problem yet unsolved. Meanwhile, let
those looking forward to the pastoral office seek to
know something of the embarrassments and trials,
the infirmities, and oppressive melancholy, that often
burden the hearts of men. A word in such a
season, fitly spoken, how good it is—how it serves
to quicken the languid energies, and give new life
to the sinking soul! In addition to knowledge,

experience is demanded. The trials and poverty which the disciples of Christ endured in common with their Master, versed them in the lore of human suffering, and enabled them to weep with those who wept, as well as to rejoice with those that rejoiced. They not only brought forth "things new and old" from the treasure-house of God's word, but each disciple had his own treasure of heart experiences, which he had been gathering all his life, and to which he was daily adding. There was thus a deep practical acquaintance gained of the human heart, which is not within the province of schools or colleges to yield—of inestimable value in dealing with men of like passions with themselves. The struggles and temptations which, by Divine grace, they had surmounted in former years, taught them how to guide and counsel others when treading difficult and dangerous ways. It is thus at the present day that the truth is to be brought tenderly home to men's hearts. "We want," says a living professor, "no more undecided ministers; but men of courage, men who hold clear opinions, men who have a strong sense of duty, and who will not shrink from doing or saying what they think to be right both in docrine and in life."

Palm Tree Christians.

"*The righteous shall flourish like the palm tree.*"
—PSALM xcii. 12.

The palm tree, among the trees of the Orient, occupies a proud position. Sacred trees—trees of life—kings among grasses—princes among vegetation—servant of God, and friend of man;—these and similar titles have been lavished upon it by historians and naturalists of every age. Nor are the royal honors bestowed upon the palm tree undeserved. They are kings not only in name. Says a living writer:—"Their claim to such distinction rests not alone on chronicles and title-deeds of old. Each freshly-springing leaf bears the very impress of royalty—weaving itself instinctively into the mighty diadem of green, the weight of which no meaner tree could support. In beauty, strength, and worthiness pre-eminent, the palm tree bears its crown right royally. Kingly, indeed, are its attributes: stately and strong, upright and unchangeable, with majestic grace dispensing, as from an inexhaustible treasury, the richest gifts unsparingly."

The palm tree, though apparently a native of the East, has also taken root in Western soil. The new world now exceeds the old in the number and variety of its palms. Europe, Asia, Africa and Australasia, contain three hundred and seven known species, while America alone boasts of an equal number, to which new ones are constantly being added. European travellers and men of science have narrated in glowing language their discoveries, and enriched our cabinets with innumerable specimens of this noble tree. The Crystal Palaces of England, and Art Exhibitions of Continental cities, contain "the crown captives of South American forests, side by side with those of Indian islands and Arabian deserts. English ears may now catch, amidst the rustling leaves of imprisoned palms, whispered memories and proud recollections interchanged between the date palm of the Arab, the Bible palm of centuries ago, and the beloved palm of the South American Indian,"—which he worships as a god.

Every Bible student, and every student of natural history, is aware of the frequent mention of the palm tree in Scripture. As far back as the days of the Patriarch Abraham, when the five kings put to flight the kings of Sodom and Gomorrah, taking Lot a captive, we read of "Hazezon Tamar," or the felling of the palm tree. In the book of Exodus we read that at Elim, one of the stations of the Israelites between Egypt and Sinai, there were twelve wells of water and three score and ten palm trees. In the account of Moses' mysterious death upon Mount Pisgah, as contained in the last chapter of Deuteronomy, we read that among the numerous places of interest that God showed His servant, was Jericho, the City of Palm Trees. At his feet, a magnificent array of palms extended three miles in length and eight miles in breadth, from whence gleamed forth the white walls and crowning towers of the proud City of Palm Trees— type of that fairer city he was about to enter. In the Book of Judges we find mention made of the famous palm tree between Ramah and Bethel, where dwelt the Prophetess Deborah, one of the Judges of Israel—a tree and a spot long reverenced afterwards by the children of Israel, in grateful recollection of her wise judgments and signal victories. Solomon takes the palm tree as an emblem of the Beloved. "How fair, how pleasant art thou! —this thy statue is like to a palm tree." It was in Bethany, house of dates and village of palms, where Mary and Martha lived, and Lazarus, whom Jesus loved. There He found a home and a place of rest from His arduous labors and long journeyings. "Heart weary and footsore, after long days of thankless toil, peace awaited Him at Bethany." On the occasion of Christ's triumphal entry into Jerusalem, also, the people took branches of palm trees, and going forth to meet Him, cried "Hosanna." And, finally, in the book of Revelations, the glorified of all nations are described as clothed with white robes and having palms in their hands: "Lò, a great multitude, which no man could number, of all nations, and kindreds, and people, and tongues, stood before the Lamb, clothed with white robes, and palms in their hands." These palms are the emblems of victory. Death has been spoiled and vanquished, and immortality possessed. The early Christians spoke of a martyr's death as "winning the palm." "They saw in the neverdying tree a type of resurrection, and laying a palm branch on the breast of every one who died in faith," declared their confidence in a future and more glorious existence.

> "A whisper, too, from worlds unseen,
> Hath the bright leaf of evergreen;
> Of realms beyond the setting sun,
> Where, when Life's busy day is done,
> Crown and palm branch shall await
> Each conqueror at Heaven's gate."

Such frequent mention of one out of the many trees which adorned the forests and gardens of Palestine cannot be entirely fortuitous or accidental. Says the Psalmist, in the ninety-second Psalm, "The righteous shall flourish *like the palm tree*— those that He planted in the house of the Lord shall flourish in the courts of our God. They shall bring forth fruit in old age; they shall be fat and flourishing." Mahomet, also, the false prophet of the east, takes the palm tree as a type of the good and generous man. "Like the palm tree," says the Koran, "the virtuous man stands erect before the Lord. In every action he follows the impulse received from above; and his whole life is devoted to the welfare of his fellow-creatures." The palm tree thus affords a fit subject of meditation to every child of God, and a means of profitable instruction in regard to the elements of Christian character. Nor is it difficult to understand why the good man is compared to the palm tree: although the appropriateness and beauty of the emblem was better understood by the inhabitants of Palestine, who were intimately acquainted with the properties and growth of the palm. Among the prominent characteristics of the palm tree of Scripture may be mentioned the great height to which it attains—its perfectly erect growth and its leafy crown, which is always green and flourishing. Not only does it seem natural for the palm tree to grow heavenward, but it is almost impossible to force it in any other direction. Other trees, when young, may be bent or inclined at the option of the husbandman, but not so the palm tree, which scorns all attempts to bias its upright tendencies. It may be burdened with weights, storms may beat upon it, and tempests wrestle with it, but it will not be bent or warped into any crookedness. We are also told by naturalists that it is most fruitful when most abused, and that the blows that bruise and wound it only increase the quantity and improve the quality of its golden fruitage. Long continued rains and floods of water do not drown it; the rays of the tropical sun neither make it wither nor decay;, from year to year, and generation to generation, it continues to grow in beauty and in strength. It is also noted for its usefulness and intrinsic value, in addition to its beauty and verdure. The date palm is a prolific fruit-bearer, a single tree yielding some four hundred pounds of dates a year. The fruit becomes to the inhabitants of Egypt and Persia the staple food upon which they subsist. Humboldt tells us that in the Brazils whole races exist upon a single species of palm, like insects which subsist on one species of flower. It was this fact that called forth the wonder and admiration of Sir Walter Raleigh, who said, "The palm tree alone giveth unto man whatsoever his life beggeth at nature's hand." Every part of the tree is of value, more or less. The leaves, six or eight feet in length, are used as coverings for the sides and roofs of houses, and for baskets and mats, and other articles of household ware. In some cases, a single leaf will cover fifteen to twenty men, and shelter them from the rain. When the sun is hot, it shades them from its heat. Soldiers on the march carry palm leaves with them on all occasions. Keeping, them dry from rain upon the journey, they make their tents for them to lie under in the night—a marvellous mercy, as has well been remarked, upon a poor and naked people in the rainy country of Ceylon. The sacred records and legal documents are written upon palm leaves. The fibrous part of the leaves and tree are made into thread and cordage, while the more solid supply fuel. The sap, when thickened, becomes sweet and palatable as honey, and the seeds when ground or broken feed the camels of the Arab. But time would fail to specify what the palm tree affords to meet the wants of man. Sugar, and fruit, and flour, and oil; wine, and milk, and bread; clothing of all kinds; ornaments for the outer, and medicines for the inner man; implements and utensils for every purpose of domestic life. So enthusiastic are the Orientals in their appreciation of the palm tree, that they enumerate no less than three hundred and sixty distinct uses to which it may profitably be applied. It is no marvel, then, that the Psalmist David, when selecting some object in nature best fitted to symbolize a good man's life, should at once have chosen the palm tree; and that Christian writers long after David's time should have made the same use of it again and again. As one of them well says, "Most fitly is the life of the Christian likened to the palm, in that the palm below is rough to the touch, and enveloped in dry bark; but above it is adorned with fruit fair even to the eye; below it is compressed by the enfoldings of its bark, above it is spread out in amplitude of beautiful greenness. So is the life of the elect—despised below, beautiful above. Down below it is as it were enfolded in many barks, in that it is straightened by innumerable afflictions; but on high it is expanded into a foliage, as it were, of beautiful greenness, by the amplitude of the rewarding."

We remark, then, that Christians are like the palm tree in respect to their beauty. The palm tree in the desert is a most grateful sight to the poor weary traveller. All around may be bleak and

barren, scorched with drought and heat, but the
palm tree remains ever green, shady, and luxuriant,
to a good old age. Although the flowers of the
tree are less remarkable than the fruit, still the
flowers of the palm tree are lovely, and their
fragrance charming. Passing through the different
stages of pure white, cream color, and pale gold,
like the dazzling colors of the rainbow, they present
a constant study to the cultured eye. And so, in
a desert, dreary world, where there is so much sin
and so much that is unlovely, the finest sight to
look upon is a godly man. The beauty of holiness
which encircles the whole person far surpasses all
the mere human gifts and graces which adorn the
natural man. The material grandeur and beauty of
the world around us deserve our admiration, but
"that is by far the best part of beauty which a
painter cannot express." Nay, oftentimes it is the
case that those outwardly most beautiful in their
persons are most unlovely in their lives. Meekness, gentleness, long-suffering, unselfish devotion
to the cause of God and truth, these are the
elements of moral beauty, and, wherever found,
command the admiration of the world. For the

beauty of Christian character, although it cannot be so readily recognized and applauded by ungodly men, nevertheless commands a certain measure of respect and esteem from the otherwise unappreciative world. Such lives are a perpetual joy and inspiration. They breathe the perfume of heaven upon the poisonous atmosphere of earth, and silently curb the evil passions of a sensual and grovelling world.

Christians are like the palm tree in respect to their fruitfulness. Beauty is not enough to make a man a child of God—faithfulness is demanded. A tree may be beautiful and fair to look upon, but barren, or the fruit it bears be unable to meet the wants of man. But not so with the palm tree. It bears in all seasons, and to a good old age. For three score years and ten, the ordinary age of man, the date palm continues yielding fruit. The blossoms on a single spathe are twelve thousand, and the fruit furnishes food for tens of thousands in Egypt and Arabia. Its fruitfulness equals its beauty. And need I say that in Christian character these are always joined. In common language we often speak of characters in the world that are beautiful and lovely, but the beauty never goes forth into actual contact with the miseries and sorrows of a fallen world. Such beauty is indeed wasted on the desert air. But the real beauty and attractiveness of Christian character consist in constant efforts for the cause of Christ and the good of humanity. The fruits of a sanctified life appear in greater likeness to the Saviour and more persistent and unwearied labors for the salvation of souls. The leaves of the palm tree do not constitute its chief value, nor do the mere leaves of a religious profession constitute a real Christian. These may receive the applause of men and deceive the company of believers on earth, but they cannot receive the reward of the Judge—" Well done, good and faithful servant; thou hast been faithful over a few things, I will make thee ruler over many things: enter thou into the joy of thy Lord." Christianity is more than theory—it is a daily life and practice. It is more than subscription to a creed and adherence to a form of church government—it is personal consecration to the cause of God. " Pure religion and undefiled," says the Apostle James, " before God and the Father, is this, to visit the fatherless and widow in their affliction, and to keep himself unspotted from the world." Only such can receive the joyous welcome, "Come, ye blessed of my Father, inherit the kingdom prepared for you from the foundation of the world. Verily I say unto you, inasmuch as ye have done it unto one of the least of these my brethren, ye have done it unto me."

Christians are like the palm tree in respect to their upward growth. The palm tree seems to raise its head as far as possible above the earth, and as near as possible towards heaven. The wax palm of the Andes attains the height of one hundred and ninety feet. In the East Indies they reach the height of twelve hundred feet. "Upright as the palm tree," is a proverb among the Arabs of the present day. And in this respect what a beautiful emblem have we of what should be the character of the child of God. His body may be bent—his mind may oftentimes sink under the pressure of severe trials and afflictions, but the aspirations of his soul, and the higher affections of his nature, all rise heavenward. As the flowers seek the sun so does the true believer the beams of the Sun of Righteousness. Nor is it wonderful that the believer should have such longings after immortality. *Here* he is but a pilgrim—*there* he will be a permanent dweller, and go no more out. *Here* he is from home, *there* he will be at home. *Here* he is an exile, tabernacling among strangers, *there* he will form one of the family circle, and take his place as a member of the heavenly household. His treasures are all *there*. His life, hid with Christ in God, is *there*—the secret sources of his renewed nature all emanate from the throne above. "All things in nature are moved and brought to their proper place by gravity, the light upwards, the heavy downwards, but the gravitation of the rational soul is love." In other words, Christ is the great attraction of the believer in heaven. His feelings are beautifully expressed by the poet:

> "Rise, my soul, and stretch thy wings,
> Thy better portion trace;
> Rise from transitory things
> Towards Heaven, thy native place

> Sun and moon, and stars decay,
> Time shall soon this earth remove,
> Rise, my soul, and haste away,
> To seats prepared above.
>
> * * * * * *
>
> Rivers to the ocean run,
> Nor stay in all their course,
> Fire ascending seeks the sun;
> Both speed them to their source.
> So a soul that's born of God
> Pants to view His glorious face,
> Upward tends to His abode,
> To rest in His embrace."

And therefore, says the Apostle Paul, "if ye then be risen with Christ, seek those things that are above, where Christ sitteth at the right hand of God. Set your affections on things above, not on things of the earth. Our conversation is in heaven; from whence also we look for the Saviour —the Lord Jesus Christ—who shall change our vile body, that it may be fashioned like unto His glorious body. For we are no more strangers and foreigners, but fellow-citizens with the saints and of the household of God."

Christians are like the palm tree in respect that its growth is in proportion to its age. It never leaves off bearing, and its last days are its best days. When the character of the wicked is portrayed in Scripture, they are said to flourish like the grass, which is green in the morning and fades before the evening. They are like the chaff which the wind driveth away. "I have seen," says David, "the wicked in great power, and spreading himself like a green bay tree. Yet he passed away, and lo, he was not; yea, I sought him, but he could not be found." All this indicates the worthlessness of the sinner's profession—the transitoriness of his best resolutions, and the sudden desolation that marks his end. But the godly man is like the tree planted by the rivers of water, that bringeth forth fruit in his season, and his leaf never withers. The man that trusteth in the Lord, and whose hope the Lord is, "shall be as a tree planted by the waters, and that spreadeth out her roots by the river, and shall not see when heat cometh, but her leaf shall be green; she shall not be careful in the year of drought, neither shall cease from yielding fruit." Such is the character of the righteous. Grace increases with age, work becomes more and more delightful as years pass on in the service of

Christ. Sacrifices are less hard to bear, and self-denial becomes a luxury, that others may enjoy the blessings of salvation. Herein mark the difference between a man who is genuinely converted by the Holy Spirit and the man who imagines himself to have experienced a change of heart under the influences of mere emotional excitement and external enthusiasm. In the latter case there may be, to the superficial observer, all the marks of true devotion to the cause of Christ, in some cases excelling the calm, steady, and silent efforts of the humble disciple.* But we have only to wait until a few years roll on to see the radical difference between the attainments and labours of these respective professors. In the case of the formalist, the flash of enthusiasm has died out, the fire of zeal

---

* A gourd, says an Eastern fable, climbed the tall stem of a palm. Having reached the summit, it mockingly questioned the royal tree,— "How long have you taken to reach this height?" "A hundred years," replied the palm. "What think you then of me?" said the gourd. "In a few days I have reached the same height that you have required so many years to accomplish." "I think nothing of that," responded the palm, "for every day of my life I have seen a gourd wind itself about my stem, as proud and self-confident as thou art, and as short-lived as thou wilt be."

and devotion has expired, the efforts that characterized the early days of church membership are no longer visible, until, by degrees, every indication of vital piety has disappeared. Instead of continuing palm tree Christians, pointing constantly towards Heaven, and having the branches full of clusters of ripe fruit, they remind us of stunted pines and dwarf oaks, which grow best on thin and sandy soils, or, like the low-lived and creeping vines, that never lift themselves above the surface of the earth. Of such it cannot be said, "they bring forth fruit in old age, and are fat and flourishing." They are of no value to the visible body of believers, and of no service to the world. On the other hand, the sincerity of the godly is proved by their perseverance not only in personal holiness, but in active labour. They are never weary of well-doing. They never feel satisfied with what they accomplish. Every new attainment is made the starting-point of something higher. If, by reason of growing age and infirmities, they cannot follow after the same employments in the Church of Christ that belonged to earlier years, then their very sick-chamber becomes a hallowed spot, radiant with the sunshine of heaven, and a source of instruction and profit to all who share their society. Thus their path is like to the shining light, shining more and more unto the perfect day.

Christians are like to the palm tree inasmuch as its greatest growth is in the most adverse circumstances. The seasons have no effect upon the palm tree. Storms and tempests, heat and cold, are no drawback to its fruitfulness; they rather seem to increase it. There is a wonderful elasticity and buoyancy in its fibres, that overcome all attempts to destroy its vitality. The more vigorous the growth, the stronger the downward pressure it has to resist. The palm was chosen in Greece as a type of the true athlete, "one never to be cast down." This strength to bear up against outward assaults is due in great measure to the firmness and depth of its root. It holds fast its root *in every soil* where it is planted, in the shifting sand and flooded plain, and barren rock, and mountain steep, as well as in the wooded valley's rich alluvial soil. "The hurricanes of tropical climes, as mad giants in their fury, buffet on every side, and forests are bowed down or torn up by their roots, but still one stately tree stands erect. The palm, unshaken and secure, will not bow or bend." And is it not so with the believer? Christ dwelling in his heart by faith, and rooted and grounded in love, enables him to overcome the bitterest forms of adversity. The fiery furnace of affliction, the crosses and disappointments in his spiritual experience, and the heavy rod of chastisement, are all so many aids to spiritual growth and fruitfulness. Strong faith in God's unvarying goodness can not only help the believer to rise superior to every obstacle that lies in his heavenward path, but changes them into blessed instruments for his advancement in holiness. How many of God's children can say, as they look back upon their history,—

>"I sought not out for crosses,
>I did not seek for pain;
>Yet I find the heart's sore losses
>Were the spirit's truest gain."

Christians are like the palm tree inasmuch as, like the palm tree, they are planted in God's house. In the building of the temple by Solomon, great use was made of the palm tree. He carved all the walls of the house round about with carved figures of cherubim and *palm tree*. The two doors also were of olive tree, and he carved upon them carvings of cherubim and *palm trees* * * * and spread gold upon the cherubim and upon the palm trees. The two doors of the temple were of fir tree, and he carved thereon cherubim and *palm trees* and open flowers. And the greater house he ceiled with the fir tree, which he overlaid with fine gold, and set thereon *palm trees* and chains. In the vision of Ezekiel, also, concerning the spiritual temple, the palm tree is represented as ornamenting the posts of the gates, and walls, and the doors. The temple was made with cherubim and *palm trees*, so that a palm was between cherub and cherub; and every cherub had two faces, so that the face of a man was toward the *palm tree* on the one side, and the face cf a young lion toward the *palm tree* on the other side. From the ground unto above the door were cherubim and *palm trees* made, and on the wall of the temple. No doubt in both cases the palm trees are intended as types of the righteous, "placed side by side with the shining angels that stand before the throne of God." The *palm tree* was also planted in the courts of temples and palaces, and in all high places of worship. There seen by the congregation of worshippers, it was not simply an object of admiration, but it suggested the patience and well-doing of the good man's life—his happy end and glorious immortality. And where, save in the Church of God, are we to find palm tree Christians? They are planted there—the sanctuary is their natural element,—God's house the place of their abode. Here they enjoy the fertilizing streams of Divine grace, and grow up into the likeness of their Master. Once they were like the wild olive, growing on the barren heath, but they have been transplanted by the Heavenly Husbandman, and are now become trees of righteousness, the planting of the Lord's right hand. And just in proportion as such Christians abound in the Church does it fulfil its great mission to the world. Where they are few, spiritual famine prevails. *Judea has now no palm trees.* A few years ago a solitary palm tree might be seen near Jericho, but that last remembrance and relic of the past is gone. Like the Jew, banished from his own beloved land, so is it with the palm tree. The curse of Israel's unbelief has fallen upon the ground as well as upon the inhabitants. Let us pray that in and around our different Zions palm tree Christians may abound, beautifying the courts of God's house, and blessing all who come under their shade.

Finally, Christians are like the palm tree inasmuch as the palm tree has an inward growth. The forest trees of temperate regions increase in size "by *external* deposition" of the woody fibre next to the bark, but *palm trees* have an inward growth. So it is with the Christian. Whatever external evidence of greater holiness and meetness for Heaven appears in his life is due to the growth of grace within. The good man is always better than he appears to the world. The secret of his perseverance in welldoing is due to the hidden influences of God's spirit continually operating upon his soul. "What means this," said Christian to the interpreter, as he was led into a place where was a fire burning against the wall, and one standing by it always casting much water upon it to quench it; yet did the fire burn higher and hotter. "The fire," replied the interpreter, " is the work of grace that is wrought in the heart." So he had him about to the backside of the wall, where he saw a man with a vessel of oil in his hand, of the which he did also continually cast (but secretly) into the fire. "This is Christ," said the interpreter, "who continually, with the oil of grace, maintains the work already begun in the heart, by the means of which, notwithstanding what the devil can do, the souls of His people prove gracious still. And—in that thou sawest that the man stood *behind the wall* to maintain the fire—this is to teach thee that it is *hard for the tempted to see how* this work of grace is maintained in the soul."

> "An *inward growth*, from the heart's crystal fount,
>   Pure thoughts, like pearl-like drops, still welling forth,
> Unseen themselves, yet swelling the amount
>   Of outward graces and intrinsic worth.
> Flourishing as the *palm*—the crowned tree—
>   Uprising in whatever lot assigned,
> Bearing the promise branch of victory,
>   Servant of God and friend to all mankind."

An Immortality to be Desired.

"The righteous shall be in everlasting remembrance."
—Psalm cxii. 6.

Unless in a few cases of aggravated crime, the actions of wicked men are buried with their bodies in the grave. The instincts of our common humanity, joined to the decree of Heaven, oppose the perpetuation of their memory. If friends are so unkind and foolish as to raise memorial stones upon their graves, inscribing thereon the names of the departed, and ascribing to them a long catalogue of virtues they never once possessed, it only renders their memory the more despicable, and makes the judgment of posterity the more severe. Bad as the world is, it cannot after death tolerate the flatteries and falsehoods bestowed upon wicked men while living. The universal feeling of our race declares that silence and the shadow of death, and the darkness of the grave, befit the open and shameless transgressor of Divine and human law. The name of the wicked shall rot—their memory shall be cut off from the earth; so the word of God testifies, and such our experience verifies.

The motives that compel men to practise virtue and abstain from vice, are many; not the least the place they shall hold in the estimation of their fellow men after they have passed away from their society. It is vain for men to say that they are totally indifferent to the opinion of their neighbours, and that, once laid in the grave, what matters it whether blessings or cursings fall upon their sepulchres. No man living, I venture to say, desires his memory utterly to perish from the earth. Even criminals, on the eve of execution, have been known to express a wish to be remembered. We dread the thought of posthumous disgrace. We want a reputation after we are gone as well as while we are alive. "As it is not pleasant to the living to think that their bodies after death shall be torn by dogs, so it is not pleasant to the living to anticipate that their names shall be infamous in the generation following." It affords no small comfort in a dying hour to know that we shall be missed and mourned; that sometimes the eye of the living shall moisten with tears at the recollection of the dead. Indeed, we have strong hope of the man who desires to be remembered by those among whom he has lived and laboured ; whose feelings are those of the poet, in lines that are immortal :

> " When I beneath the cold, red earth am sleeping,
>   —Life's fever o'er,
> Will there for me be any bright eye weeping
>   —That I'm no more ?
> Will there be any heart still memory keeping
>   —Of heretofore?
> When the great winds, through leafless forests rushing,
>   —Like full hearts break :
> When the swollen streams, in crag and gully gushing,
>   —Sad music make ;
> Will there be one, whose heart despair is crushing,
>   —Mourn for my sake?
> When the night shadows, with the ample sweeping
>   —Of her dark pall,
> The world and all its manifold creation sleeping,
>   —The great and small :
> Will there be one, even at that dread hour, weeping
>   —For me, for all ?"

This, perhaps, my hearer may say is nothing but sentiment. If so, it is sentiment founded upon reason, in accordance with the purest sympathies of our nature, and founded upon the word of God. For, in addition to the hope of immortality through the death and resurrection of Christ, the Scriptures everywhere assert that after death the name and memory—the good actions and holy life—of the upright man shall be a constant power in the world. Being dead, he shall speak to coming generations. His name is not simply chronicled in Heaven, but long after his bones have mouldered in the grave, and the stone that bears his name has crumbled into dust, his memory shall be fragrant in the world. On the other hand, it is asserted of the wicked man, that his name, his descendants, his memory, his birth-place, his death-chamber, and his grave, shall be forgotten, or, at best, but remembered with loathing and disgust; while the piety and virtuous actions of the good man shall be revered and honoured—embalmed in the affections of universal humanity!

What then, it is asked, are the conditions of true fame—of a glory and renown that fades not with the decay of matter; that waxes brighter and brighter as ages roll on, and Time gives place to Eternity? Not greatness, in the ordinary sense of the term, but goodness; not intellectual power, nor riches, nor royal parentage, but love of God, a pure and gentle heart, a disposition child-like and humble, a walk and conversation governed and directed by the indwelling spirit of Almighty God. These are the essentials of immortality on earth; these are the best of all guarantees that our memory shall not be forgotten when we pass away to the rest and rewards of Heaven. Such an immortality every one may inherit. It is given to but few to have their names inscribed in the nave of Westminster Abbey, or to have a niche assigned them among the poets and warriors and statesmen who in past days have adorned the commonwealth and blessed the world. But it is within the reach of the humblest member of society to perpetuate his memory in a way more enduring than sculptured marble or gilded bronze. "They that be wise shall shine as the brightness of the firmament, and they that turn many to righteousness, as the stars, for ever and ever."

It is taken for granted that every man desires to be remembered after death. To be forgotten, like the pebble cast into the sea, that scarce causes a ripple upon the surface of the water, is not a comforting or pleasing thought to an immortal soul. If such, my hearer, is your desire, how do you expect to be remembered? Are you labouring day and night to secure a large amount of material good? Are you seeking after a position of power and influence among your fellowmen? Are you covetous of the honours of statesmanship? Are you exerting yourself in behalf of the commonwealth of which you are a member, in the fond expectation that your name and memory shall be ranked with patriots and benefactors whose lives have been devoted to the accomplishment of great and mighty projects of social reform? In a word, are you depending entirely upon your outward acts and public deeds of self-denial for this posthumous immortality?

We do not despise nor undervalue any one, or all, of these avenues to immortality. But a word of caution is necessary, that you do not place undue dependence on one, or all combined. Mere riches cannot give immortality. It is true they may command at death mock mourners, and all the outward pomp and display which so often accompany the rich man to the grave; they can secure a costly mausoleum and a marble tablet over the decaying dust; but this is all they can effect. Mere riches, apart from moral worth, never yet perpetuated the memory of any man. On the contrary, riches, unused for God's glory and the world's good, but hasten what may be called moral annihilation—immediate and entire forgetfulness after death. Have you not seen this again and again exemplified in the community where you dwell? Men of reputed, and, it may be, real wealth, have passed away as if they had never lived. Save in the cemetery, where a tombstone records their age and resting-place, their remembrance is blotted out from the memory of the living! People say of such men when they die,—" No loss to the world; but few will miss them"—if they do not indeed publicly execrate their memory and hold them up to the scorn of coming generations.

Scarcely more substantial or certain is the posthumous immortality which is founded upon the opinion of society: the gratitude—or rather ingratitude—of kingdoms and republics, in whose behalf men so often spend their lifetime, in hope of undying renown and imperishable laurels. One false step, one political error, however unintentional and undesigned, serves in many cases to blot out the record of a faithful and honorable career, and to shatter the expectations of many years. The applause and favor of the mob is at best but fickle and wavering. The idol of to-day is the despised and insulted creature of to-morrow—but a football for the passions of an ignorant and excited populace. Have you not seen men of the most straightforward principles and reliable morality rejected by constituencies for nothing but manly adherence to conscientious dictates? But even were it otherwise, what, after all, is the fame and immortality that follow statesmanship or political success? At best it is but a poor substitute for that lasting renown which a life of goodness secures to its possessor; not for a moment to be compared with the fragrant perfume which proceeds from holy acts —which makes the grave a sweet resting-place, and death the beginning of a better and more imperishable existence.

There is no member of this Church, it is to be hoped, who does not desire to leave his children some heritage—some memorial of his love and some tribute of his affection. Houses and lands, silver and gold, apart from hallowed recollections of the dead, are but poor memorials indeed. But poor as they are, comparatively few of us have even these to leave to those we love. To meet the daily calls of life is all that the major part of society can accomplish, and even this much with a hard and continuous struggle. Yet let not the poor man murmur if, in the exercise of faith and piety, he leave his children the memory of a well-spent life. The son or daughter who can say, standing over the grave of a beloved parent,— "Here lies a poor but honest man"—is rich indeed—heir to a better fortune than the gold of India or California. There is nothing so comforting in the hour of trial, when children are called to part with beloved parents, as the consciousness that no man can accuse their memory of wickedness, or call up the blush of shame to the mourner's cheek. That is a far better portion than marble palaces and stately mansions, built upon the gains of fraud and the grinding of the poor. Such a legacy the poorest man can leave behind. By a blameless, holy life; by industry and sobriety; by love to man and fidelity to God, every man can leave behind a memorial infinitely more precious to his family than broad acres of land or the coronet of a peer.

In view of all this, is it too much to say that every man is the architect of his own monument, and that it is within his own power whether his memory shall perish after death or remain a source of happiness and strength to coming generations? These remarks are specially applicable to young men—to those on the threshold of life and called to face its temptations. The desire of fame is strong in youth. To rise superior to the mass of men, and secure a niche in the world's gallery of heroes, is the dream of millions. One seeks for immortality by pouring out his soul in poetry; another by the discoveries of science; another by commerce; and still another at the Bar or in the Senate. Goodness is too often a secondary consideration, provided the end considered all-important is reached,—to sit as a king upon a throne, and hold a sceptre of intellectual power over the lower classes of humanity. And yet how few reach the summit of worldly greatness! How many who cry "Excelsior" reach the Alpine heights! A few years ago a volume of poems was published, the writings of a Scottish boy who died ere he reached the age of 24.* It contains little that can be considered the higher inspiration of the poet's lyre, but is full of that burning desire after immortality so characteristic of youth. Writing to an English poet he says:—"I tell you, if I live, my name and fame shall be second to few of any age, and to none of my own. I speak thus because I feel power." Leaving his quiet village home for the great English metropolis, we find him walking through Westminster Abbey, friendless, and almost penniless, yet eager for this posthumous immortality. "I am in London," he writes again, "and dare not look into the middle of next week. What brought me here? Westminster Abbey! I was there all day yesterday. If I live I shall be buried

---

* Poems by David Gray: Roberts, Boston.

there!" But it was otherwise ordained. Consumption, that takes away so many of the young, laid hold of his system, and speedily dragged him to the grave. "The vision darkens," he writes. "My crown is laid in the dust for ever. *Nameless, too! How that troubles me!* Had I but written one immortal poem, what a glorious consolation! But this shall be my epitaph, if I have a tombstone at all:—

> "'Twas not a life;
> 'Twas but a piece of childhood thrown away."

Poor David Gray! One over-mastering passion, the ever-burning desire for fame, swallowed up every other in his bosom, and were it not for lines here and there scattered over his remains, we might be ready to say in reading his life,—"Vanity of vanities, all is vanity." There is hope, however, of one who wrote—

> "There is life with God,
> In other kingdom of a sweeter air;
> In Eden every flower is blown."

To sum up all that we have written: Goodness, not greatness, is the only certain pathway to immortality. When combined, they constitute a glorious life, but if we cannot reach the latter, let us by all means secure the former. The shortest biography on record is the most honored:—"Enoch walked with God, and he was not, for God took him." How much is included in these brief words! Humility — gentleness — purity — separation from the world—likeness to Christ—and zeal for His glory. We live in an age when such solid virtues are undervalued. Gifts, not graces, are now reckoned valuable. Men esteem the favor and applause of the multitude of more account than the esteem of Heaven. On all hands busy brains are at work seeking eminence in the world; but how few, by patient continuance in well-doing, strive after honor, glory, and immortality? Such glory is worth the living for; is praiseworthy to seek after, and certain to be enjoyed if consistently pursued. It is held up before us as an incentive to noble actions; as a spur to quicken our flagging energies; and as more than a recompense for the trials of the present scene. Ye humble and holy workers for the good of your fellow-men, be comforted by the thought that you are not and cannot be forgotten.

You who from day to day are toiling and doing noble acts without seeking the praise of man; you who are living like the Master, and bearing untold sorrows without disclosing them to your fellow men; you who are poor and despised and unknown:—do not fret or murmur because of your obscurity. You belong to Christ. Your dust is precious in His sight. After death, He will not only keep your bones in safety until the resurrection morn, but he will make your name and memory sweet in the ears of living men. When the military hero dies, the nation mourns. A thousand chimes of bells wail the tidings to the people, and poets sing his praise. But when a good man dies, Heaven secures His immortality. Angels strike their harps, and joy pervades the ranks of the redeemed. The real heroes of the world lie in graves marked by no monuments, but their memory pervades society as the atmosphere girdles and permeates every nook and corner of the globe. Dying they begin to live—completing those grand and noble projects which the world despised when first conceived. John Bunyan, Richard Baxter, Wilberforce, Jonathan Edwards, Whitfield, Wesley,

Knox, Luther, Chalmers, Guthrie, and such men, are better known and more highly esteemed than when they lived. We miss their bodily presence, but we feel the mighty grasp of their spiritual power that rules the world. Though dead, such men speak, and are held in everlasting remembrance.

A New Year's Greeting.

"𝔅𝔢𝔩𝔬𝔟𝔢𝔡, 𝔍 𝔴𝔦𝔰𝔥 𝔞𝔟𝔬𝔟𝔢 𝔞𝔩𝔩 𝔱𝔥𝔦𝔫𝔤𝔰 𝔱𝔥𝔞𝔱 𝔱𝔥𝔬𝔲 𝔪𝔞𝔶𝔢𝔰𝔱 𝔭𝔯𝔬𝔰𝔭𝔢𝔯, 𝔞𝔫𝔡 𝔟𝔢 𝔦𝔫 𝔥𝔢𝔞𝔩𝔱𝔥, 𝔢𝔟𝔢𝔫 𝔞𝔰 𝔱𝔥𝔶 𝔰𝔬𝔲𝔩 𝔭𝔯𝔬𝔰𝔭𝔢𝔯𝔢𝔱𝔥."—3RD EPISTLE OF JOHN, 2.

At this season of the year the exchange of Christian greetings and good wishes for each other's welfare is eminently fitting. Human life, in its brightest moments, has enough of trial and disappointment, without foreshadowing or anticipating coming evil. To enjoy, in a spirit of sincere thankfulness, the mercies bestowed upon us from day to day, and go forward hopefully to the unknown future confident of the protection and favour of Heaven, are the dictates of enlightened faith.

The beloved apostle John presents us with a fine example of such a Christian greeting. " Beloved, I wish above all things that thou mayest prosper and be in health, even as thy soul prospereth," is his earnest prayer for his near and dear friend Gaius. Apart from the inscription of the Epistle, we can almost trace the author by the loving language and simple style of the sentence. There is a certain indescribable graciousness and affection about all the writings of John, found in none other of the Apostles ; a tenderness of expression which became sweetened and softened as years increased. Having shared largely in the love of his Divine Master, he is earnestly desirous that this same love may be visible in all the members of the Christian Church —that their affection for each other might be so conspicuous as to win over a sceptical and ungodly world. " He is the mirror of love. He had been so often with his Master, and leaned upon His bosom, that like men who have lain in beds of spices, he had the perfume of delight upon him." Love was the never-varying theme of his sermons, and the sum of what he wrote and acted out in life. Not contented with writing to the early churches in their collective capacity, and exhorting them to the practice of charity, he seems to have written private letters to such of their members as enjoyed his personal friendship. Gaius was one of these friends, and in all likelihood the same as Paul mentions, in his Epistle to the Romans, as a man of unbounded hospitality to the disciples and servants of Christ. The same noble testimony is borne to his character by John in this letter. " Beloved, thou doest faithfully whatsoever thou doest to the brethren and to strangers; which have borne witness of thy charity before the Church." It was not ostentatiously to display his resources, or to secure the good-will and favour of his fellow-men, that he so acted. He was a man of ardent piety, not ashamed to recognize and affiliate with the despised followers of the Nazarene, and not afraid to shelter all who came under his roof. He was one of those great and large-hearted men that Providence raises up in every age to be almoners of Heaven's bounty to the needy and distressed, and helpers to His church.

It is such a man whose welfare John desires, and nothing can be more beautiful than the phraseology employed. It is just as if he said,—" I wish that in all things temporal you may be as prosperous and successful as you have been in things spiritual." It is not a simple wish for the health and happiness of his friend, but that his outward prosperity may be proportioned to his inner joy, and "that the current of his outward life may flow on smoothly as the course of his spiritual being." In the estimate of the Apostle, no man should seek worldly advancement in advance of genuine piety and the fear of God. Where the balance is not thus carefully adjusted, it is bad for the man himself and injurious to society at large. The great law of Christian ethics is, "Seek ye first the kingdom of God and His righteousness, and all these things shall be added unto you."

We gather from John's prayer for his friend Gaius—

First: That the grace of God in the heart is not of necessity incompatible with the possession of wealth and influence. Gaius was, in a worldly sense perhaps, "a great man," but he was at the same time "a good man." He had not only secured of this world's goods what enabled him to disburse liberally for the glory of God, but he had received into his heart the true, imperishable riches, which no change of condition or estate could alienate from his person. It is allowable for us also to suppose that he had found the pearl of great price —the one thing needful—before that Providence had so largely blessed him with temporal prosperity. In too many cases riches come into the possession of sordid, penurious, and avaricious men, who are ignorant of the first principles of Christian stewardship, and the end for which such a talent is entrusted to their keeping. But in the case of Gaius, the heart was first made rich with the love of God before that his gains increased. He was thus enabled by heavenly wisdom to use his influence and estate for the good of men and the highest interests of Christ's kingdom upon earth.

Second: It is only such men that can be safely entrusted with the elements of power and abundance of riches. It needs a large supply of grace in the heart to keep the head from becoming giddy when fortune smiles upon us, and the world begins to flatter. It is wrong to desire for any worldly man great outward prosperity. It is neither for his own good nor the interests of his fellow men that he should possess power and position while destitute of that inward satisfaction which is altogether independent of external circumstances. No sight in the world is more melancholy and pitiable than to see men outwardly gay and happy, while strangers to the pure and imperishable joys which spring from holy living. Riches, in the possession of such men, have a direct tendency to harden the heart and deaden the spiritual powers. Under the scorching sun of worldly prosperity, whatever there is of natural goodness and generosity of soul is sure to dry up and wither, until the man becomes entirely the creature of sense and the slave of unholy passions. Instances are innumerable where men's souls have become petrified by years of uninterrupted prosperity. Without the restraining influences of God's grace, the heart becomes insensible alike to all manifestations of Providence, whether of love or judgment. As business increases—as wealth gives men a conspicuous importance in the eyes of their companions, and as they begin to feel themselves of some consequence in the world—they look with growing indifference on the state beyond the present; if indeed they do not become practical sceptics, living without the knowledge of God here, and destitute of desire to enjoy Him hereafter.

Third: The measure of worldly prosperity that any one should wish for himself and others is to be regulated by the state of his soul. As the soul prospers, but not otherwise, are we to desire outward prosperity. If this be a true principle, what would the effect of such prayer, if answered, have upon the outward condition of many professing Christians? If instead of wishing our friends, in common phraseology, "a good New Year," and "the compliments of the season," and "health and wealth and happiness," we were to qualify our greetings with the words, "as thy soul prospers," would it not reduce some of the richest and most respectable men to abject beggary? From being looked up to as the honorable and exalted of the earth, they would be despised and forgotten in their poverty and obscurity, and if our bodies were only to enjoy health and vigour in proportion as our souls were in such a condition, would not many of us spend years on beds of languishing, without a moment's rest from pain and sickness? Such a prayer would in effect be to many the invocation of a curse rather than a blessing. "How few of us would be outwardly bettered—on how many would the outward change be shocking to behold! Let the body be as the soul is, and how many who are now seen in youth, and health, and comeliness of aspect, would instantly assume the withered and wasted look of age! How many would become forms and shapes from which the eye with instinctive disgust would turn away." Yet this is the rule of Christian life, as laid down in Scripture. Whatever endangers the soul's welfare; whatever cools our spirituality; whatever lessens our interest in the affairs of Christ's kingdom; whatever, in a word, puts in jeopardy the welfare of the soul, is to be carefully avoided, no matter what may be the apparent sacrifice. "What shall it profit a man though he should gain the whole world and lose his own soul; or what will a man give in exchange for his soul?" Religion must keep pace with— nay, should be in advance of—every outward blessing we enjoy. If we do not grow in grace as we succeed in business, and grow strong inwardly as we flourish outwardly, then the cup of our prosperity will ultimately become the instrument of our perdition.

A New Year's Greeting.

One of the first sermons preached by the writer of these lines was to a congregation, one of whose members had but a few days before been elected to the Congress of the United States. He was a man of marked ability, and had occupied almost every position of honour in the church and community where he resided. Descended of a godly family, his father having for many years presided as an upright judge, this man had been the subject of many prayers, and, up to that time, had nobly fulfilled the highest expectations of his friends; nor is it known to the writer that he has ever deteriorated from the high standard of principle and piety so early set before him. But his pastor was anxiously solicitous for his spiritual welfare, regarding the political honors conferred on him as bringing to an end his usefulness in the church, and leading to his spiritual decline. It should not be so, it may be replied, and it is not always so, but in very many instances rapid advancement in material good is the precursor of moral ruin. Such fears all ministers have, more or less, for souls in whose eternal welfare they are interested. For, explain it as we may, no one can deny that the Church of

Christ is most largely indebted for unflagging zeal and effort to her poorer members. When our attachment to this world, so far as riches are concerned, is little, the heart goes forth untrammelled and unshackled to the work of preparing for the next. When our capital in earthly things is small, our interest in spiritual realities is large.

These remarks are not intended to produce a spirit of indifference in regard to the welfare of the body, or the necessary demands of material life. There is, indeed, little danger that men will either recklessly squander their health away, or fail to take advantage of openings in the commercial world that promise large returns for the capital invested. The Apostle himself did not undervalue such things. On the contrary, he prayed that his friend Gaius might enjoy health and prosperity. Health of body is a prerequisite to soundness of mind. Without health, no continuous labour can be comfortably carried on, either in the secular or religious world. Worldly prosperity is also a lawful object of ambition, provided we retain the mastery over the wealth acquired, and do not allow the soul to fall down and worship it. But beyond these, and of vastly more importance, the health of the soul is to engross our earnest attention. We are to be jealous of every indication of declining piety, and watch over its alternations of feeling with more interest than the physician watches the changing countenance of his patient and notes the beating of the pulse. If the heart throb faintly—if its action is so weak and sluggish and irregular that it can hardly force the blood to the extremities, then life is in jeopardy. And if the soul is so feeble in its spiritual pulsations that it has no relish for unseen things, then spiritual death will speedily ensue.

Do not think us unkind, then, in view of these statements, if we do not ask for any man more material prosperity than his soul enjoys of spiritual health. Better that a man be bankrupt in purse than in soul. Better that he should have but bare supplies from day to day, than that with large endowment of this world's favors, his soul should be poor toward God. Real wealth consists not in houses and lands, in gold and silver, but in faith, in love, in humility, and Christian contentment. Such wealth becomes part of the man and enters into the very essence of his moral being. It cannot be filched away by thieves, nor depreciated by the quotations of the stock exchange. It cannot be lost by accident, nor is it left behind at the hour of death. It lasts through infinite ages—imperishable and indestructible. And if, in the case of a Christian, we should not and cannot ask for more, what shall we say of those whom God has blessed with health and wealth and outward prosperity for many years, but who have never once realized their indebtedness to Providence, and never experienced a single grateful emotion? We may not perhaps wish that God would suddenly strip them of all those things they so highly prize, but we cannot certainly desire that their riches may be increased. "As soon wish that fuel may be added to the raging fire, or fresh lading to the sinking ship—as soon wish that treasures of gold may be cast into the sea, as into the cold, thankless, all-engulphing selfishness of an ungodly heart."

How many men, then, who are outwardly prosperous, may be in what physicians characterize as a most critical condition in so far as the health of the soul is concerned! It is with them the crisis of the disease. The fever has reached such a stage that it must either kill or be conquered. More than ordinary applications are needed in such cases to restore spiritual health. Unless God's omnipotent power produces serious and solemn concern, the issue will be fatal throughout eternity. The goodness and long-suffering of the Almighty seem to produce in many cases callousness and indifference to what should be the chief concern of every immortal soul. The continuance of unbroken health, and every material good that can minister to social happiness, seem to lead some men to run riot amid the pleasures and pastimes of the passing hour. Like the rich man in the parable, they say: "What shall I do, because I have no room where to bestow my fruits? I will pull down my barns and build greater, and there will I bestow all my goods and my fruits. And I will say to my soul, Soul, thou hast much goods laid up for many years; take thine ease; eat, drink, and be merry." How foolish such conduct, when, as we know, the present life is, after all, but an insignificant part of man's existence! The excitements and pursuits of the present can do nothing to allay those pangs of despair which the soul must feel which has missed Heaven in grasping earth. Have you, my reader, ever taken stock of your soul's wealth? You have stated periods in your business arrangements for calculating profits and losses—seasons when you institute the most rigid scrutiny into your monetary affairs, lest in the hurry of life some element fatal to your prosperity should enter unperceived. Does not true wisdom dictate a similar investigation into the health and vigour of the soul?

Let young men, especially, learn from these remarks what kind of prosperity is most desirable, and should enlist their earliest attention. The common idea is, this world first, and heaven next; business now, religion afterwards. The practice is to give to the world the best days of existence, and what remains to God. "When I have established myself in business," says the young man, "and acquired a certain amount of capital, and can command leisure to think seriously of such weighty matters as the salvation of the soul, then I will set about it in earnest; but don't talk to me at present of anything beyond my daily occupations." What does such talk mean? "When I can no longer take the same interest in the world—when I come to be a poor, broken-hearted and brokendown old man, incapacitated for bodily and mental effort, I will then devote to religion the time that hangs heavy upon my hands, and endeavor to make up for past neglect." Just as if the Almighty had given a lease of life for so many years, and in the event of existence thus prolonged, would accept of such a mean and contemptible conversion! The man who deliberately gives to Satan the morning and manhood of his life, has no right to expect mercy in old age or in his dying hour.

Some who read these lines have been greatly blessed above their fellowmen with worldly prosperity. What, let me ask, are you doing for Christ in proportion as God has increased your stores? Are you giving in proportion as your means increase? Are you dedicating of your substance to the extension of His church in the world, and the glorifying of His name? This is what Gaius did.

He was a succourer of many. The early Church met in his house, and the poor afflicted Christians never came to his door in vain. He gave liberally, and worked earnestly for the spread of Christianity in the world in an age when self-denial was a daily and hourly practice. How much more should Christians of the present day, who enjoy luxuries and comforts altogether unknown to the primitive Christians? What will money and possessions do for any man when lying at the gates of death? Nothing but increase the agony of the dying hour, and fill the soul with unutterable dread at the thought of meeting the Omniscient Judge? "Give an account of thy stewardship, for thou mayest no longer be steward," is a summons often addressed to men in the very prime of manhood, and absorbed in the gains of commerce. To such how significant are the words of Christ,—"If ye have not been faithful in the unrighteous mammon, who will commit to your trust the true riches?"

What, it may be asked, are the elements of soul prosperity? The elements of worldly prosperity are generally considered to be health, wealth, and power; success in business or professional life; influence over our fellow-men, and possession of their favour. The elements of soul prosperity are spiritual and symmetrical growth—the active exercise, the gifts and graces made over to every believer in Christ by the indwelling of the Holy Spirit; a deeper piety and unfeigned humility; a greater indifference to things visible and tangible, and a growing meetness for Heaven. A man may be a believer—saved by grace and certain of eternal life, and yet by no means spiritually prosperous. Many men in commercial life manage, by hard fighting and unceasing struggles against misfortune, to live and maintain their credit, and support their families in some small degree of decency and comfort, but they are by no means what men call prosperous. They do not enjoy existence—it is to them a drudgery and source of constant anxiety. The matters that demand daily attention are, what they shall eat and drink, and what they shall put on. How to meet their payments and satisfy their creditors are questions that force themselves upon the mind by day and by night. And so there are many good men in all our churches who simply live. The flame of the Divine life exists, but nothing more. The light is dim and flickering—not clear and bright. They are at the best but timid, weakly and sickly children in the family, in constant need of care and nursing. They are, for some reason or other, never perfectly assured of their own standing in Christ, and cannot testify to others of the riches of the kingdom. "What a hospital," says a living writer, "is many a church? Here lies one poor man, down with a paralysis of faith. Here is another, laid up by a sprain which he got by a sudden fall into temptation. Here is one whom the fever passion has burnt out, and looking hardly worth the medicine to cure him. Here is another under pastoral treatment for the blindness of unbelief, and another whose gaping wound reveals the spot where Satan's fiery dart went in! And here, too, is a whole dozen who skulked into the hospital to get rid of the draft from Sabbath schools and mission labours."

Now, in opposition to such weakness and infirmities, a prosperous soul is sound, healthy, and vigorous. He has got beyond the rudiments and first principles of his faith. He can give to all men a reason for the hope that is in him, and declare to others the secret things of the kingdom. He experiences even now that joy which is unspeakable and full of glory. There is steady progress in Divine attainments. All the powers and affections of the soul grow harmoniously and in equal proportion. In many Christians there is a distorted, one-sided growth. Some one grace overshadows all the others. The spiritual strength that should be impartially distributed, through all the members, seems concentrated in one. There is nothing of that beauty and completeness of Christian character described by the Apostle Paul when he says, "till we all come in the unity of the faith, and of the knowledge of the Son of God, unto a perfect man, unto the measure of the stature of the fulness of Christ." This however is the normal condition of a really prosperous soul. There is enlightened judgment, untiring zeal, fervent devotion, outspoken profession, unfeigned charity and cheerful liberality. In a word, a healthy Christian is a whole man, ever able and ready to take his part in the great enterprises of the church, and give his aid in the evangelization of the world.

Such a condition of heart is surely worth the having. It can be attained and enjoyed by diligence and dependence upon the grace of God. If men would take half the pains to secure soul prosperity that they put forth to possess material good, how different would be the condition of the Christian world! Success in business is dependent upon perseverance, industry, unflagging purpose and devotion to daily duty, and spiritual prosperity is acquired by the use of all the means provided for the culture of the soul. It has been wisely remarked that there must be constant attention to little things. The soul, as well as the mercantile establishment, often makes a failure solely through its neglect of these. There must be a reliance upon one's daily, regular, habitual work, rather than a looking for sudden and unexpected gains. "It is not what the soul does occasionally under great pressure, nor what it learns or receives at rare intervals, that sets it forward in true prosperity, so much as what it does from abiding principles and from a controlling purpose of life daily pursued. And, finally, there must be common sense—which is worth as much in securing the soul's prosperity as it is in making a fortune."

The Master's Call.

"*The Master is come, and calleth for thee.*"
—John xi. 28.

"Why not sooner?" Mary might naturally have responded when her sister Martha exclaimed, "The Master is come, and calleth for thee." The time was past when they most needed and desired His presence. They had sent for Him, but He had not come. Day after day they had looked anxiously out of the window of the death-chamber, expecting the approach of their well-known and welcome Friend, until hope died within their breasts, and the sorrow of bereavement dimmed their eyes with tears. Now all was over! Lazarus was dead, and had been buried. Of what avail Christ's coming now? Nothing, but to open afresh the flood of emotion, and give occasion for bitter regrets that He had not sooner come to the help of these lonely sisters. The language was, "If Thou hadst been here, my brother had not died."

And so we reason, in our moments of despair, when the billows of the Almighty overwhelm us. Because our prayers are not answered in the way we want them;—because the power of the disease is not broken, and our friends restored to health;—because we are made to pass through dark and mysterious Providences without the felt presence of the great "I Am," we mourn and complain at God's absence, and call in question His love and friendship. We forget what the incident before us clearly teaches, that the sympathy and consolation of Heaven is as much required in the days that *follow* bereavement as in the dying chamber; that it is when the heart begins to feel its loneliness, and, realizing the awful blank that has been made, seeks in sad and melancholy musings to perpetuate its grief, that then, most of all, do we need the presence of Christ and the consolations of religion.

But Mary did not so speak. Sorrow-stricken though she was, she firmly believed that "He had done all things well," and that for some good reason He had come at last; and, therefore, as soon as she heard the words of Martha,—"the

Master is come, and calleth for thee,"—she arose quickly and came unto Him.

God never sends affliction or bereavement into a Christian family without some special end in view. As regards the individual, we may be sure the trial is necessary—while a loud call is addressed to all the members and friends of the family circle. We may not at the time be able to trace the meaning of His afflictive dispensations, or believe that love and mercy are mingled with each and all; but there is no cause to doubt the declarations of Scripture, that "whom the Lord loveth He chasteneth," and "scourgeth every son whom He receiveth," and that He doth not willingly afflict the children of men. We cannot, in the present case, tell why the friend of Christ, whose character bears no stain whatever, so far as narrated, was subjected to weary days of painful agony, and finally to pass through the darkness of the grave; but we can rest assured that in his case, as in the case of the bereaved sisters, some high purpose was accomplished, and some useful lesson taught. It was to improve the sad event, sanctify the death, and prepare them for the speedy resurrection of their brother, that Christ now approached the house in Bethany, where often in former days He had been a welcome visitor. He came not simply to weep with those who wept, and sympathize with the broken-hearted, but to inspire with a nobler faith, and to impart the better consolations of His grace.

I remark then, that in times of severe affliction and bitter bereavement, the Master *calls us to commune with Him.* He would have us leave behind weeping relatives and mourning friends, and seek the retirement of the closet, where, alone with our Maker, we may unburden our hearts and learn His will. Mary had often before this sat at the feet of Christ, and enjoyed profitable communion with Him. While her sister Martha was busy with the duties of the home in Bethany, Mary preferred to hear the Master discourse of Divine and eternal realities. But in these days no sickness marred the even tenor of their way—no shadow crossed their path—no gloom or melancholy interfered with their innocent enjoyments. Happy in each other's society, and favoured with the presence of the

Saviour around their humble board, they seemed specially exempted from the misfortunes and the calamities more common to the world, and had no special call to muse upon the lessons of mortality so long as the family circle was unbroken.

But all this is now changed. Mary must enter upon another department of study. Alone with Christ she must be taught the reasons of God's mysterious dealings with her, and be led more submissively to acknowledge His goodness and bow to His will. The Master had come, and now called her to impart such knowledge as she had never yet learned, nor could possess save in close communion with the Saviour.

We are called, then, in times o distress, to nearer and more intimate fellowship with Heaven than in the usual conditions of a religious life. It is presumed that every child of God enjoys communion with his Maker in every season of existence, and that without such companionship his spiritual life would decline and languish. But we need occasionally to withdraw from the common surroundings of the family and Christian society, and, alone with Christ, talk of unexplained and mysterious Providences that cause us no little mental anxiety. Mary must leave Martha behind when she would commune with Jesus. She had her own singular thoughts and feelings which no one else could understand; her own difficulties which no one else could remove but the Master. Much rejoiced we cannot doubt she was when she heard her sister say, "The Master cometh, and calleth for thee."

Do I not speak the experience of God's children when I say that amidst the common employments of life and when all things are prosperous with us, we often neglect secret communion with God? The pressure of business—the cares of the family—the endless official engagements that demand our attention from week to week, leave us little time for meditation—for silent, secret prayer, and calm undisturbed communion. We all feel this,—we lament it; and yet when some startling and severe calamity comes upon us, intended to arouse us from our carnality and summon us to closer fellowship with God, instead of regarding it in this light we murmur and repine at the cruel judgment. How few of us, brethren, save when laid aside by sickness, have an opportunity to review our past life—to examine our hearts—to ask ourselves the question, most solemn and important, how we stand towards God and eternity! How seldom, save when called to the bedside of the dying, or the house of mourning, or the grave-yard, do we sincerely contemplate our latter end!—and even then it is but a passing reflection. When the grave has been filled—dust to dust, and ashes to ashes;—back again to our homes, and engrossed among the cares of the world, we too soon forget the lessons that such oft-repeated sights are intended to impress upon the mind. But when the little child is laid low in death, and the cradle is left empty, and its innocent prattle is no longer heard; or when the blooming son or daughter is snatched away in the opening years of life and hope; or when the husband or wife is taken from the centre of the household;— then we are compelled to turn our thoughts inward, and enquire into the reason of God's dealings with us. When the windows are darkened—and the bell is muffled—and the soft footsteps of enquiring friends and sympathisers are heard in the room of death, and we feel *alone* in the world, and for the first time realise what death is, as we stand before the silent remains of beloved friends;—then we feel there is only one we can converse with. "The Master has come, and calleth us."

But I remark, again, the Master comes at such seasons and calls us *to experience His sympathy and receive Divine consolation.* Mary and Martha were not altogether friendless in Bethany; the narrative shows the reverse. They and their brother were held in high esteem. We cannot doubt but that during the illness of their brother, and after his death, many enquiring Jews were seen approaching their home, tendering their loving services, and doing what they could to mitigate their sorrow. Blessed be God, human sympathy is not limited to any one nation or kingdom. The rude, uncivilized barbarian that lives in the desert, shows, in his own peculiar way, that he can feel, and sympathize, and weep with friends who weep. But the bereaved sisters, accustomed to the tender tones of a nearer and dearer friend than could be found among the circle of their relatives, were only mocked by the common forms of grief, and the usual accompaniments of Oriental sadness. They would far rather be left alone, in solitude and tears, to brood over their severe affliction, and perpetuate their sorrow.

It is worthy of notice that Christ came to sympathize and console, not at the very moment of bereavement, but after some days had elasped. Lazarus had been buried, and the mourning sisters had returned to their desolate home. Purposely— as we learn from His own words—He had remained absent until the present hour. There was doubtless good reason for such conduct. There are times when we want no sympathy whatever; when the kindest attentions of friends are a burden, and their presence an intrusion. Grief must have its outlet— the overflowing heart must have unrestrained freedom in giving expression to its grief. We do not want the usual commonplace, and, shall I say, ill-advised visits of well-meaning friends, who know but little of our condition, and but increase our anguish. We feel it better to sit in sackcloth and in ashes, and weep beside our dead, than see the face of any living being. Surely the affliction has been sent for this, among other reasons, that alone we may commune with our own hearts, and taste the full bitterness of bereavement. We shall welcome the tender words of friends, who have experienced similar bereavements, after time has been given for the outgushing of our emotions; but till then let not the silence be broken.

But a period comes when we need sympathy and consolation. We must not remain disconsolate--weeping as those who have no hope. The heart yearns for companionship. Gradually we can bear the beams of light in the darkened chambers of the soul, and seek for words of sympathy and consolation. Then, oh how gratifying the tidings, "The Master cometh, and calleth for thee!" We would not undervalue the real sympathies of Christian friends who speak tenderly of Jesus and His compassion. We delight to hear of that Great High Priest, who, touched with a feeling of our infirmities, has pity for us in all the ills of life,—but above all this, we would see Jesus Himself. We would like to hear from His own lips the Divine consolation which is His alone to offer. Silently we would pillow our head upon His bosom, and sink into His arms of love. He knows us as no other possibly can; the precise condition of our minds—the part of our emotional nature that most needs succour; what truths and promises are best fitted to restore us to our natural calmness, and make us triumph over Death itself. He has wounded, and He alone can bind up;—He has chastised, and He can heal;—He has dimmed our eyes with tears, and He alone can dry them.

We cannot, as Mary and Martha, hear from Christ's own lips those consolations of His grace that are so well fitted to cheer our sinking souls. He no longer stands by our open graves, weeping with us at the loss of our friends. But His glorified humanity in Heaven is still cognizant of our earthly agonies. He is as ready, and as able to comfort, as when He entered into humble cottage homes, and talked with bereaved friends. Ere He left the world, He promised the disciples that He would send "the Comforter," who in periods of despondency and grief would minister to their wants. And there are times when we are thus made sensible of "the Master's call," in and through the operation of the Spirit upon our hearts. Have we not all felt how certain passages of God's word, borne in upon our spirits in moments of heaviness, have exercised a power and produced results altogether singular and inexplicable;—changing our feelings, banishing our doubts, tranquilizing our fears, and mitigating our sorrows. We have been conversant with the same truths for years, and have heard them repeated again and again by ministers and friends, but never before have we grasped their fullness. In the light of our affliction they possess a sweetness, an adaptedness,—a wealth of comfort never before understood. We feel that it is wrong to mourn and murmur. The trial has been sent in mercy, and we are able to say "Thy will be done."

But, finally, on this point I remark, that in such seasons the Master calls us *to behold greater revelations of His power and goodness*. Martha had great confidence in the Omnipotence of Christ to raise her brother from the dead, but we can hardly believe she expected so much. She knew that whatever He asked of His Father in Heaven would be granted, and she looked forward to the resurrection, when her brother would rise, as Christ seemed to hint in His conversation. But an immediate restoration to life was more than she could hope for. Had He come sooner He might have averted the final issue, but now that the blow had been struck, there was nothing but submission to the mysterious decree of Heaven.

But Christ had designs of mercy with these sorrowing sisters far beyond their expectations. He would assert His claims to Divinity as He had never done before, and, in the recalling of Lazarus from the grave, would astonish and convince the most incredulous Jew. It was not singular He should desire to see the place where His friend was buried, and, standing over the grave's mouth, pronounce some words of hope. But more than this He purposed in His present visit to Bethany. And so we read that, when He came to the grave, He commanded that the stone should be taken away, and after lifting His eyes in prayer to His Father in

Heaven, He cried with a loud voice, "Lazarus, come forth." Straightway the dead came forth,— the blood began to circulate in the veins—the eyes to beam with intelligence, and the tongue to speak. "Loose him and let him go," said the Saviour, and Lazarus, leaving behind him for a time the gloomy prison of the grave, was restored to his beloved sisters. Such a wonderful manifestation of Christ's power and goodness they had never before witnessed during all the previous years of intimacy and friendship.

Now, in seasons of distress the Master comes, and calls us to witness similar manifestations of His power. He does not literally bring back our friends to life, but He does what is of equal value. He brings us to regard them as not dead but living; as only removed from sensual vision, but still palpable and real to the grasp of faith. And need I say what wonderful relief the stricken soul experiences in this comforting thought. The first feeling that comes with the sight of death, is the breaking up of associations and friendships, cemented and strengthened by years; the end of hopes and fond desires; the sundering of attachments that formed the very essence of our enjoyment in the present world. It is very true, that believers in the doctrine of a future state and a glorious resurrection to everlasting life, ought never to regard death in such a gloomy light. But in spite of the Christian's creed, the possibility of such eternal separation, and kindred thoughts, unscriptural though they be, will torment the mind and agitate the soul beyond endurance. It is not until a certain measure of calm reflection has been obtained that we are able to overmaster our fears,—to silence the sceptical suggestions of our material nature, and to feel that the dead are with us still, only in the enjoyment of a nobler and purer existence.

But passing from such thoughts, more immediately springing out of the text, I add that there is a time near at hand, when it shall be said *to one and all of us*, "The Master is come, and calleth for thee." To some, *that will be the hour of death*, and how soon none of us can tell. We have no guarantee that life will be lengthened by a single day, or that we shall have timely warning of our end. To how many does the Master come suddenly and unexpectedly; in the enjoyment of health and vigor, and with every indication of a long and useful existence. To others the call will come *at the Second Advent.* "Behold I show you a mystery; we shall not all sleep, but we shall all be changed in a moment, in the twinkling of an eye, at the last trump; for the trumpet shall sound, and the dead shall be raised incorruptible, and we shall be changed." We shall not all die, or enter the grave. There will be found, when Christ comes in glory to judge the world, numbers of the human family, who shall simply be transformed so as to fit them for the life of Heaven. "We which are alive and remain, shall be caught up together with them,—(the dead in Christ) to meet the Lord in the air, and so shall we ever be with the Lord." It is useless to speculate as to the time of Christ's coming. Far more important is it that we should be ever prepared for that event. As in the days of Peter, so now—there are to be found many scoffers, walking after their own lusts, and saying, "Where is the promise of His coming? for since the fathers fell asleep, all things continue as they were from the beginning of the creation." The delay is not reason for doubt as to the fact. The Scriptures emphatically declare it. The world demands the coming of the Lord. The entire creation groans and labours under the burden of sin. Our own reason and conscience call for a day when rectitude and justice shall be manifested to the living and the dead. "The Lord is not slack concerning His promise * * * The day of the Lord will come as a thief in the night; in the which the Heavens shall pass away with a great noise, and the elements shall melt with a fervent heat; the earth also and the works that are therein shall be burned up." But to all the call will come *at the Day of Judgment*. Whether our bodies have reposed for ages in the grave, and our souls have for a like period inhabited the spirit-world, or whether body and soul are to be instantaneously changed so as to fit us for appearing at the bar of God;—to all of us it shall one day be said, "The Master is come, and calleth for thee." The call is to a solemn and final investigation of life's work—to acquittal or condemnation—to hear—each one for himself and herself—the impartial sentence of the Great Jehovah. From that dread bar there is no escape. Every eye shall see the great white throne, and every ear shall hear his doom.

The call to many of us—come in what form it may, and at what time it may—shall be unexpected and sudden. As it was in the days of Noah, when the flood came upon the earth, so shall be the Master's call. Hence the necessity of constant preparedness. Are your affairs settled with your Maker? Is your calling and election sure? Have you the lamps trimmed and burning, and the loins girt about? Are you ready to welcome the bridegroom when He comes, and go in with Him to the marriage? Business men at certain seasons of the year, are found balancing their books, closing their accounts, examining into the true state of their affairs, testing their solvency, and arranging to meet pecuniary demands that press upon them. Are you doing the same in regard to the more important affairs of the soul? Have you settled your accounts with your Maker? Are you ready at any moment to render an account of your stewardship? Are you living, from day to day, under a realizing sense of your awful nearness to the Eternal World, and the dreadful interests that are at stake, when Time, for you, shall be no more?

Now, in order that you may conscientiously answer such questions, let me suggest a few practical thoughts worthy the solemn consideration of every hearer of the Gospel. Have I, during the past year, improved the many privileges that a merciful God has put within my reach? Have I availed myself of the outward means of grace, and presented myself before the Lord when the doors of the Church have been thrown open? Have I engaged in the devotions of the sanctuary under a recognition of the Master's presence, and with a strong determination to benefit by the spoken Word? And have I prefaced and followed my Sabbath day exercises with earnest prayer for God's blessing? I fear many of us cannot answer those queries satisfactorily to ourselves; far less if standing in the presence of the Judge of all the earth. Again, ask yourselves what attainments in holiness—what large and accurate views of divine truth, and what clearer conceptions of your acceptance and peace with God, have you reached? Or, if you would prefer the testimony of the life, rather than the experience of the soul, then take honest account of your past actions. What have you accomplished during the past year for the good of humanity, the glory of God, the extension of His cause and the hastening of His Kingdom upon the earth? Have you cheerfully responded to the many calls in Providence that have been addressed to all who profess to be followers of Christ? Or, have you, on the plea of inability, worldly occupations, or mere want of inclination, turned a deaf ear to these entreaties? However much we have accomplished, the best must feel how insignificant have been their aims, and how poor their achievements. But, oh! how dreadful must be the retrospect of an utterly wasted and fruitless year.

To many families in this Church, during the year now closing, the words have been addressed—"*The Master is come, and calleth for thee.*" To those of us mercifully exempted from the shadow of death, the call is just as loud and personal. We are members one of another, and when one member suffers, all the other members suffer with it. We cannot predict who shall next be called into the presence of the Judge, or what family shall first be made to feel the chastening rod! Year after year new breaches are being made; the faces of friends disappear from our ranks, and the grave encloses all that is mortal from our view. Blessed be God, we know that this is not the end of human friendships. After Mary had come to see Christ He said unto her, in order to calm her fears and strengthen her faith in His power to quicken the very dead: "Said I not unto thee that, if thou wouldst believe, thou shouldest see the glory of God;" and forthwith that glory was manifested far beyond her expectations. We still wait a similar display of Almighty power. Concerning them which sleep in Jesus we sorrow not even as those which have no hope. "For if we believe that Jesus died and rose again, even so them also which sleep in Jesus will God bring with Him."

Touching His Garment.

"*She came behind and touched His Garment.*"
—MARK v. 27

The miracle wrought by Christ upon the poor woman afflicted with an issue of blood, is one of the many evidences the Scriptures afford of Christ's readiness to do good at all times—to the bodies as well as the souls of men. This woman, to use the language of common life, was cured by incidentally meeting Christ on His way to raise the daughter of Jairus. While He is addressing the Pharisees, as we learn from the context, this ruler comes to Him, beseeching Him to come and see his child, who is lying at the point of death, if not dead already. On His way to the house of Jairus, this poor woman presses through the crowd that follows Christ, touches the hem or border of His garment, and is instantly cured. Meanwhile, the daughter of the rich man—the possibility of whose recovery seemed to depend upon Christ's immediate presence —has died, to the great distress of her mourning friends, and the evident annoyance of on-lookers, who imagine that Christ's presence is no longer of any avail. Better, doubtless such people thought, for Christ at once to have hastened to this desperate case, without allowing Himself to be delayed by this poor afflicted woman. But Christ thought differently. Possessed of infinite resources, He could as easily raise the dead as cure the dying; and so, on His way to raise the maiden, He heals this aged sufferer. In His eyes, though poor, her life was just as precious as the daughter of the ruler.

Let us look briefly at this poor woman's case, and next at her faith, as expressed in the words of our text—"She touched His garment." She had been long afflicted with the issue of blood; for twelve years she had never known what it was to be free from pain. She had, during that long period, tried many a pretended cure, and spent all her living upon physicians, without receiving any relief. Nay, we are told she rather grew worse under the repeated changes of treatment to which she was subjected. Her malady had become chronic, and doubtless she often felt that there was no cure for it but the grave. And so it would have been but for the timely arrival of the Saviour, whose wondrous displays of grace and power were not entirely unknown to this poor woman. By what means she was apprized of Christ's approach we are not informed, but one thing we know, that she lost no time in hurrying towards Him. As Satan said concerning Job, "Skin for skin, yea, all that a man hath, will he give for his life." She had nothing more to give, but if cured at all by Christ, she knew it would be free. She does not stop this wonderful physician and state her case. She rather shrinks from His presence, desirous of stealing a cure without the knowledge of the Saviour. The crowd is great, and at first it would seem as if it were folly for this poor, enfeebled, wasted creature, to attempt to touch Him. But in proportion to the weakness of her body is the strength of her faith. "If I may touch but His clothes," she says, "I shall be whole;" and this, at whatever peril, she is determined to effect. So, with wondrous pertinacity, and the putting forth of what to her was supernatural strength, impelled by a force of will that overcomes all obstacles, she presses in behind, touches His garment, and straightway finds the fountain of her blood dried up. Her body is healed of the plague that has so long dragged her down to the grave. This secured, she desires nothing further. Satisfied with a bodily cure, she has as yet but little conception of the far worse malady that is wasting the soul. But Christ will make the cure complete. He must teach this poor woman more of His character and His love than she has ever yet learned, and therefore He says, turning about on the crowd, "Who touched my clothes?" The act, unperceived by all but Christ, and known only to the timid, shrinking woman, who now comes trembling to His feet, must carry with it far greater results than she had ever intended. And so we read, when she had told Him all the truth, instead of administering rebuke, He said unto her, "Daughter, thy faith hath made thee whole; go in peace, and be whole of thy plague."

Now, apart from the plain declaration of Christ, I can easily fancy that we should characterize this woman's act as mere superstition rather than efficacious faith;—akin to the act of the poor deluded

Romanist, who imagines that kissing the crucifix in some way secures exemption from bodily diseases or the guilt of sin; or that of the High Church Ritualist, who places dependence on mere external ordinances rather than in the completed work of Christ. "Of what value," it may be said, "a mere touch? Whatever the result may have been, so far as the woman was concerned it was a mere delusion, a fancy, a fond, superstitious hope, altogether different from real, genuine, saving faith."

Now, in the outset, we must admit that the woman had *genuine faith*. We have nothing at present to do with its strength or the degree of its enlightenment; we simply have to do with the fact that faith existed in this poor woman. The narration of the miracle by the three Evangelists is not intended to hold her up as a specimen of faith that Christians are to rest contented with, but rather to show how little and how weak a faith may procure eternal blessings from the Son of God. That it was genuine we dare not doubt, for the cure effected was in response to her faith. Christ could not possibly mistake the woman's feelings, for He says "Thy *faith* hath made thee whole,"—instrumentally at least, if not directly.

What, then, are some of the characteristics of this faith? I answer—First: *It was an unenlightened faith.* What did she believe? Simply that in Christ there was power to cure her of her issue of blood; that if she in some way got herself into contact with the living Man—even if she but touched the hem of His garment—she would be cured. She looked upon Christ as dispensing temporal blessings unconsciously; that His will, and compassion, and Omnipotence, had nothing whatever to do with the miracles performed. She seemed to believe that the cure would be as perfect if secured without, as with the cognizance of the Saviour. I presume, that, akin to the delusions practised upon thousands many years ago, who went on pilgrimages to touch the "Holy Coat of Trenes," she imagined that in the fabric there resided the magic charm that wrought cure upon the person whose finger touched it.

Secondly: *It was a very narrow and circumscribed faith.* It sought nothing more than the cure of the body. It never imagined that the person who could, consciously or unconsciously, work such a miracle, could, in the higher region of the heart and mind, perform still greater wonders. It may be answered, with some show of justice, that the first thing this poor woman needed was the drying up of her fountain of blood, and that, probably, this accomplished, she would press for still greater blessings. There is no evidence of this whatever. But for Christ's interposition she would have secretly withdrawn, without even telling, to the crowds that followed Christ, the wonderful relief she had experienced. She wanted present health, and nothing more. She cared nothing for pardon—peace—present assurance, and everlasting happiness.

Thirdly: *It was very weak faith.* She could not face the Saviour. She was afraid that she might be repelled. She was by no means confident of His treating her case with consideration and sympathy. Had she possessed strong faith, she would have at least made known her sad condition, even supposing that the cure was possible without His knowledge or interference, and gladly poured forth her gratitude when sensible of relief. She knew nothing of that holy boldness that the apostle speaks of, which enables the believer to come to the throne of grace to obtain mercy and find grace to help in time of need,—nothing of that continued wrestling which characterized Jacob when he said "I will not let thee go except thou bless me,"— and received power to prevail over God and man.

But feeble, unenlightened, circumscribed though it was, it was nevertheless genuine faith so far as it went. It held fast by one fact, that Christ had power to save;—that her issue of blood was curable if she could but touch His garment. It was not that strong faith which unites the soul to Christ, and enables the advanced believer, casting all fears and doubts to the winds, to repose with perfect security upon His finished work. It had no respect to spiritual blessings whatever, and yet, in spite of all these defects, it was none the less genuine faith.

There are different kinds of faith, as well as degrees of faith. There is the feeble clinging faith of the

new-born babe in Christ, and the strong masculine
grasp of the experienced believer. And there is a
faith that takes hold of Christ as the source and
dispenser of minor benefits, and a faith that trusts
Him for everything the sinner needs, whether apper-
taining to the body or the soul. In many cases
this weak, ignorant, unenlightened faith precedes
the strong confidence that more frequently belongs
to maturer age ;—nay, may I not venture to say,
that often God's gracious compassion towards the
ailments of the body makes trembling sinners bold
to seek the more valuable blessings of redemption.
Many a man, who never thought anxiously about
his soul's salvation, has been brought to serious
reflection by answers given to his prayers for the
restoration of some beloved child. With that instinct,
if we may so call it, which drives the most wicked
men in times of calamity to their knees, he
beseeches the Almighty to grant the cure desired,
and bless the means employed, and, the prayer
being granted, becomes the means of leading him
to the exercise of a higher faith in God's mercy
towards lost and perishing souls. If there is faith
at all—sincere and genuine—there is hope of

increase and strength. We must never despise the lisping, stammering accents of the young convert, nor laugh at the crude and undigested ideas he entertains of the doctrine of grace and the work of Christ. The faith of the most advanced believer is, after all, nothing to boast of. In the estimation of the higher intelligences of creation, it may seem as incomplete and unsatisfactory as does the faith of this poor woman, which reached no farther than the border of Christ's garment. I am not one of those who laugh to scorn the devotee clasping the crucifix, and lying prostrate before the cross and altar which symbolize a suffering Saviour! The material crucifix and cross cannot certainly impart any lasting virtue, but who knows but the eye that seems to rest upon the cross and crucifix may pass on to the Crucified Redeemer, and rest in His active intercession with the Father rather than in the wooden symbol. By means of such representations, rude and vulgar though they may appear to the refined and spiritual worshipper, the ignorant, simple-minded suppliant may reach the heart of Christ.

Why, the faith of this poor woman seems to me wonderful, when we take into account her previous circumstances. You, who from your earliest years have had Christ presented to you as the Saviour of men's souls as much as their bodies, and who know that it was for this very purpose He came to earth, cannot realize the difficulties that Jewish or Pagan converts had to overcome before arriving at a full-orbed faith in His Messiahship. The predictions of Old Testament Scripture, concerning the mission and death of Christ, were as yet unintelligible to the great mass of the nation, and, to very many of the Rabbis, Christ was chiefly known as a wonderful miracle worker, and these miracles were all performed on the bodies of men. By the exhibition of this supernatural power He desired to establish His claims to Divinity, and gradually lead the minds of spectators to an apprehension of His sublimer attributes. All that this poor woman knew of Christ was from common report, as to His success in healing the diseased; and yet her simple faith, resting upon the truth of human testimony, led to a firm assurance of His power to relieve her of her loathsome malady. It is not likely she ever saw Christ before, or heard from His lips any of those declarations regarding His atoning work, which at later periods of His earthly ministry He made known to the disciples and the crowds that followed Him. She is not, therefore, to be blamed because her faith was not *in advance* of her knowledge; if it was *up* to her knowledge, it was far more than that of Gospel hearers of the present day.

Is my language too strong? I repeat it then. The faith the poor woman exercised is greater than the faith of many Christians at the present day, if we take into account their respective privileges. You would regard it as insulting were I to place your intelligence on a level with this poor, uneducated, ill-informed Jewess. Educated in a Christian land, and from your childhood conversant with the great facts of Christ's life and death, you are not of those who cling to the beggarly elements of a past dispensation, or restrict your faith to the mere forms and shadows of the past. Going beyond all this, you value no forms of worship but what are spiritual. You believe as much as did this poor woman in the reality of Christ's miracles while on earth, but, going farther than she did, you regard them as types of the more malignant maladies of the soul, which none but the Great Physician can eradicate. Your faith rests not in times or places, but in the all-sufficient merits of the crucified Nazarene. A truly good confession of faith, my Christian hearers, if your practice is in accordance with it; but, on the other hand, a woful testimony to your insincerity, if your faith fall below your creed! Come now, honestly let us look at the matter. You regard Christ as the great soul saver. You never think of Him but as the Anointed One, sent to preach good tidings to the meek—to bind up the broken-hearted—to proclaim liberty to the captives—to open the prison doors to them that are bound. You glory in the freeness and fulness of the atonement, saying, perhaps, in the triumphant language of the Apostle, "God forbid that I should glory, save in the cross of the Lord Jesus Christ." You have no sympathy with those who would interpose anything that is human between Christ and the sinner, whether it be Priest or Pope, or altar and censer; and yet you have never yet accepted of that Saviour as offered you in the Gospel! Nay, you have not done so much as this poor woman, who touched the hem of Christ's garment because she knew no better— never yet seriously cried, "God be merciful to me a sinner." Who, now, is the Ritualist? Who is it that is trusting in forms? Who is it that, like the Pharisee of old, is placing faith in washings, and fastings, and phylacteries, and synagogue attendance? Whose faith is the more real—genuine? Whose conduct the most to be commended? Verily I say unto you, that the publicans and harlots shall enter into the Kingdom of Heaven before you. The men of Nineveh shall rise up in the Judgment with this generation of nominal Christians, and condemn them; for they repented at the preaching of Jonas, but behold, a greater than Jonas is here!

In the estimation of Christ, her faith was precious, not, perhaps, for what it was as yet, but for what it was destined to become. What she wanted was more light; a deeper insight into the mysteries of grace; a clearer apprehension of her own wants, and of Christ's fulness. This attained, she would come to "the knowledge of the Son of God,"—to the measure of the stature of the fulness of Christ. The proof that her faith, however clouded and incomplete, was genuine, is furnished in the reply of Christ and the instantaneous cure effected. It was not, certainly, the touch of the garment that made her whole, although she thought so as yet. But it is unnecessary for the cure that Christ should enter upon a lengthy explanation of the nature of saving faith. He does not rebuke her foolish trust—her childish fancy. He does not attempt in this stage of her Christian experience to initiate her in the high things of the kingdom, but, coming down to the low level of her understanding, He gives her what she wants, and in the way she wants it. The cure comes indirectly through the robe of Christ; but the worker is the same Omnipresent, Omnipotent God, who honours the weakest faith and welcomes the humblest suppliant.

There is comfort here for the meanest and most obscure of God's children. True faith, though genuine, may be as feeble in its manifestations as was hers. Fears, and doubts, and perplexities, not so much, perhaps, as regards the Saviour's ability to save as His willingness to consider your special case; humbling thoughts of your desperate wickedness and unworthiness; all combine to make you feel at times as if you were outside the pale of God's mercy. Ah! it is not so! There is infinite fulness in the heart of Christ to meet your every want. His grace is not dispensed according to your faith, but rather according to your need. There is no necessity that you should go through a stated round of forms in order to secure an audience. Press through the crowd! Touch the hem of His garment, if all you can do, and your salvation is complete. It matters not whether it be the touch of Christ, or the touch of the sick soul, provided there is contact with the living Redeemer. In many cases cures were effected by the touch of Christ, as in our text. We are told by the Evangelist that on one occasion all the diseased in the land of Gennesaret crowded to Christ, beseeching Him that they might only touch the hem of His garment, *and so many as touched were made perfectly whole.* There are many ways by which the soul is led to

Jesus, but only one method of cure. You must *look* to the brazen serpent; you must have faith in the blood that is sprinkled upon the door-posts; you must sincerely feel like Peter when, sinking in the waters, he cried—" Lord, save me or I perish;" or like the poor leper who came and said, " Lord, if Thou wilt, Thou canst make me clean." In that case, as in the case of this poor woman, the faith was very weak and ignorant, yet omnipotent to secure relief.

> "He knew the power; the love he did not know,
> That power he sought; nor pleaded he in vain:
> The love he knew not came in fullest flow."

Oh, the blessedness of the cure! the instantaneousness of the remedy!

> "I touch Thee and am cured! No touch of mine
> Can render Thee impure! Whatever be
> The foulness of the hand that touches Thee,
> Thee it defiles not, yet it cleanses me.
>
> "I touch Thee, and the electric current flows;
> My touch has all Thy skill and power revealed;
> Thee I infect not with my sins or woes,
> And yet, by touching Thee, my soul is healed.
>
> "It gives to Thee my sickness, and to me
> Imparts Thy health; my evil Thou dost bear,
> And I Thy good; all mine inquity
> From me Thou takest; I Thy beauty wear."

Brethren, is it not true, that often we get more from God than we ask or expect? He supplies us according to the infinite resources of His grace, and not according to the limited petitions of His creatures. We come for bread to eat, and He gives us the living bread that came down from Heaven. We come for water to quench our thirst, and He gives us the living water that flows from the throne of God, and of the Lamb. We come for the cure of bodily ills, and He says: "Thy sins are forgiven thee; go, and sin no more." We come for some poor, insignificant gift, and lo! He gives us Himself. "Daughter, thy faith hath made thee whole; go in peace, and be whole of thy plague."

It has been my desire, all through these remarks, not to depreciate strong, intelligent, eagle-eyed faith, but to encourage such as possess only weak faith. We must not imagine that because weak faith is honourable in God's sight, that aspirations after stronger faith are undesirable and unnecessary. Far from it. In the infancy of a soul's spiritual being we do not expect the same heroic achievements as in its maturity; the same unclouded trust; the same unlimited reliance; the same resistless importunity. The young soldier staggers somewhat at the first blaze and thunder of cannonry that salutes him from the enemy, but the old warrior stands firm and fearless, because long accustomed to the fight. The child asks but small favours from the parent, but these increase in number and value as he reaches maturity. You, who boast of being already the people of God, do not therefore rest satisfied with the mere germs of faith! Seek after the very highest attainments in Christian experience! Have you obtained forgiveness? then seek after assurance! Have you enjoyed momentary glimpses of Christ's face and presence?—Strive to make them more frequent and abiding! Have you the graces of the spirit in your soul?—then make them evident to the world by exhibiting a faith that works by love! You are not to take for your measure this poor woman who was satisfied with the mere touch of Christ's garment, but, going on unto perfection, you are to excel in gifts and godliness. Seek nothing less than daily communion with Christ; abiding in Him, and He in you, as the source of all your real strength!

As it is, what are the facts with regard to the great majority of professing Christians? Is it not too true that we are satisfied with pardon of sin, and, in the exercise of selfishness, steal away from Christ as did the woman when she felt the issue of blood stayed? There is great emotion and apparent concern at the moment of conversion, but apathy and indifference succeed. We settle down into what are called the "sober realities of a religious life," contented with the mere existence of spiritual hopes, but without any settled determination to reach the highest excellencies and eminences of which the saint is capable on earth. And thus it happens that we possess none of the joys that accompany assurance of salvation, and are the ever-increasing victims of despair and despondency; at times bringing us to a point when we almost doubt the love of God entirely, and our saving interest in the atoning work of Christ. Brethren, this should not be. "Be strong in the Lord, and in the power of His might."

Finally, let the example of this poor woman rebuke the conduct of indolent hearers of the

Gospel, who never press through the crowd to see or touch Christ. Seasons of religious, excitement come and go; men are crying out "Jesus of Nazareth passeth by;" but they cannot be moved out of the dull uniformity of outward routine. What are you waiting for, sinner? Do I need to assure you of Christ's readiness to hear your case and administer relief? See Him hurrying along to the house of Jairus! The case is urgent, there is no time for loitering on the road; but here comes a poor sinking woman who has been many years afflicted and needs His pity. What does he do? Scorn her cry? Or rebuke her impertinence? Or leave her to die at once?—only a few years, perhaps sooner, at the most, than in the natural course of events she would. Ah, no! He stops, and as silently as she had touched His garment, frees her from the load of her wretchedness. But this is not all. He gives her such a revelation of His Divinity as makes us hope she found a better cure than that of the bloody issue. But you say, "I cannot go to Christ. Am I not taught that by nature I am unable to take the first steps, unless moved by a superior power. I am waiting like the man at the pool of Siloam, for Divine help, before I find my way to Christ." And so men fool themselves into the belief that, after all, they are not entirely to blame for their unbelief. This. doctrine of man's inability is made to do duty for all the indifference and inconsistencies that mark so many Gospel hearers. "You can't come to Christ you say." Who said you could, unaided? But you can seek the influence of God's spirit upon your soul, to quicken your flagging energies and arouse you to active effort. Make the attempt at least, my brother. If you fail you can be no worse than you are. If Christ does not hear you and help you, then by all means declare as loudly as you can the inefficiency of the world's Redeemer. But not until you have resolutely made an approach to the Great Physician dare you accuse the Almighty of inability or unwillingness to treat your case. Men may shelter themselves now behind these refuges of lies, and parry with eternal truth by thrusting such flimsy pretexts in the preacher's face. But all this self-deception ends at the bar of God. Then, if never before, you will find, in the wretchedness of never-ending torture, the infatuation

Touching His Garment.

of the soul that neglects salvation. Christ is passing by—hurry to Him—touch the hem of His garment if you can do no more, He will not rebuke thee—love and pity is in His voice—forgiveness in His eye.

"Who touched Me?" dost Thou ask;
'Twas I, Lord, it was I;
"Some one hath touched Me"—yes, O Lord!
I am that somebody.

"I came, Lord, and I touched,
For sore I needed Thee;
Forth from Thee straight the virtue came:
Lord! Thou hast healed me.

"What could I do but touch,
And Thou so nigh, so nigh?
What couldst Thou do but heal, O Lord!
Ere I had time to cry?

"And would'st Thou frown on me,
Dost Thou the boon repent?
Why then, Lord, didst Thou pass so near
As if to me just sent?

"Speak then the word of cheer,
Say to my trembling soul:
Be of good comfort; go in peace;
Thy faith hath made thee whole."

How Old art Thou?

"And Jacob said unto Pharoah, the days of the years of my pilgrimage are an hundred and thirty years: few and evil have the days of my life been, and have not attained unto the days of the years of the life of my fathers in the days of their pilgrimage."—GENESIS, xlvii. 9.

The drawing-room receptions of kings and queens are not, in general, occasions for serious reflection upon the shortness of life. The display of gorgeous apparel—the glitter of pearls and diamonds—the attendance of royal courtiers—the crowd of fair women and brave men that eagerly await the recognition of the sovereign—the hurried and formal interview prescribed by court etiquette, are all unfavourable to religious impression. Amid the gaiety and splendour of a palace seldom do men learn the lesson taught us by Solomon—"Vanity of vanities—all is vanity."

The Book of Genesis introduces us to the levee of an Oriental king—on a somewhat limited scale, it is true, compared with court presentations of the present day. The principal figure in the group, next to the king himself, is that of an aged, hoary-headed man, bent down with the weight of years and sore calamities. The old man is surrounded by his sons, the younger of whom, now prime minister of Egypt, introduces him to the sovereign. It is no ordinary presentation that we are called upon to witness. Jacob and his sons are here by special invitation. Pharoah, in token of his gratitude for the dutiful service rendered by Joseph to the kingdom, has extended them a royal welcome to make the land of Egypt their permanent residence. " The land of Egypt is before thee; in the best of the land make thy father and brethren to dwell." The temporal wants of the patriarch thus fully met for the remainder of his days, be they few or many, he doubtless feels a strong desire to see the monarch whose generosity has made such ample provision for his declining years. Nor is it too much to believe that on the part of the king the desire was fully reciprocated.

To become acquainted with the father and brothers of the man who, as chief counsellor of state, had conducted affairs in years of unparalleled difficulties, was no ordinary gratification; while to confer honour upon them, and show them more than the usual kindness and condescension of royalty, would be but the natural promptings of his heart.

What were the feelings of the king when he looked upon the venerable sire that stood before him, and what the feelings of the patriarch, it is vain to conjecture. As Jacob looked upon the heathen prince who had shown him such kindness, his heart swells with gratitude, and he supplicates the blessing of Jacob's God upon the king, and upon his land. Forgetting for the moment the dignity of the sovereign in whose presence he stands, his deep emotion carries him far beyond all formal ceremony, until he audibly lifts his heart in prayer to the God of his fathers, who had so wondrously provided for all his wants, and turned his sorrow into joy. Nor was Pharoah less overcome by the appearance of the good old man. There was something so solemn, so sincere, so earnest and unaffected in his manner; his speech was so entirely different from the customary language of royal courtiers; his appearance was so venerable— the years of sorrow through which he had passed having left indelible furrows upon his brow, whitening his hairs and enfeebling his step; and, withal, there was so much majesty and dignity in his deportment, that the king was struck with surprise and admiration. King though he be, he instinctively feels that a greater than an earthly monarch stands before him—a servant of the Most High, whose blessing was more valuable than all the treasures of his kingdom.

Old age has many claims upon the respect and admiration pf the young, more especially if it is an old age of honorable service in the cause of Christ. There are many duties we owe them; and the older they are the more attentive should we be to discharge them. Soon they will be entirely beyond the reach of our kindness and indifferent to our gratitude. There is much also to be learned by the story of our life. "Days should speak, and a multitude of years should teach wisdom." A man who had arrived at Jacob's age, and passed through so many eventful years, gaining a deep insight into human nature on the one hand, and experiencing a large amount of God's grace on the other, was most admirably fitted to give counsel, even to men who occupied positions of dignity and trust like the king of Egypt. Possibly with such feelings passing through his mind, Pharoah put to Jacob the question, "How old art thou?" Laying aside the formal words of state, and condescending to the language of familiar converse, the king would hear from his own lips some particulars of his eventful life. He already knew that Jacob and his sons were worshippers of the one living and true God, and towards this religion many recent circumstances may have turned the attention of the king, and gained for it a favourable consideration. Then he wanted still further to learn the secret of that wonderful cheerfulness and joy that beamed in the patriarch's countenance, notwithstanding his exceeding age, and how he was sustained in looking forward to the end of life.

If mere curiosity prompted the question, the king must have been sadly disappointed in the answer.

Jacob understands well how seldom, in all probability, he would stand in the presence of royalty, and how earnestly he should improve the present opportunity. He would endeavour to impress upon the king the shortness of life, even though extended to a hundred and thirty years, and the vanity of all human possessions and enjoyments. He would help him to realize that existence here, even when lavishly enriched with every comfort that can fall to the lot of man, is after all but a pilgrimage of sorrow that leads to the grave. Nor are these solemn reflections rudely pressed upon the king. With admirable tact and prudence, and in a manner at once solemn and unaffected, he replies:—"The days of the years of my pilgrimage are one hundred and thirty years; few and evil have the days of the years of my life been; and have not attained unto the years of my fathers in the days of their pilgrimage."

How strikingly do these few sentences photograph, as it were, the life of Jacob! "Few and evil" is the graphic description of his years. He had not attained the average duration of life in his ancestors, but suffering sufficient for the longest life had been his portion. Every new stage of his existence seems to have added new force to the poet's words, that "Man was made to mourn." His early and hurried flight from home to escape the vengeance of his brother Esau; the hunger, and thirst, and sleepless nights that doubtless marked his pilgrimage; the long years of service, and the fraud and treachery of Laban, practised under the garb of friendship; the dissensions of his wives, and the quarrels of his children; the shame of Dinah, his only daughter; the horrible wickedness of Reuben, his first-born and the loss of his beloved son Joseph, forcing the aged patriach to exclaim, "I will go down into the grave unto my son mourning;"—these are but specimens of the trials that had saddened his days. Was it any wonder, then, that Jacob should at times have taken a gloomy view of God's providence, and in the anguish of his soul have felt that "all things were against him!"

If honestly put, there is no question susceptible of greater profit than the question of our text, "How old art thou?" and yet there is no question we care less to answer. It would almost seem as if men imagined that by allowing their years to pass unreckoned, they prolonged their existence and delayed the approach of death. To realize that we are growing old, that our strength is daily decreasing, that the memory is less retentive, and the step is more languid and feeble—in a word, that we are no longer capable of the efforts of our younger days, and are rapidly approaching second childhood, is of all knowledge the most distasteful. Instead of calculating how many sands of the glass are run, and anticipating an early, and it may be sudden summons to the eternal world, we fondly indulge the hope that life will be extended to its utmost limit. We call up before us the names of friends still living whose age is far in advance of ours. We flatter ourselves that we have come of a long-lived ancestry, who bravely battled with the King of Terrors, and only yielded when resistance was in vain. Thus we begin new projects and lay the foundation of new enterprises, when, in the estimate of our fellow-men, the only investment that remains for us is a few feet of mother earth, and a stone to mark the resting-place of our ashes!

The pertinency of such a question will appear when we reflect for a moment upon the oft-repeated statement that life is short, even when extended to three score years and ten. *No hearer present will ever reach the age* of the Patriarch Jacob, when he stood in the presence of Pharaoh. One hundred and thirty years had already passed over his head, and nearly twenty years more were yet to run ere he should be gathered to his fathers. And yet in Jacob's estimation this was a brief existence. When a child in his father's tent, innocent and happy, with no cares or anxious forethought to disturb his dreams or shade his joys, his estimate of life was very different. The hundred and thirty years, that now seemed but a few days in retrospect, would then seem immensely long—more than enough to satisfy every longing of his soul. And so it is with every one who has reached or passed the age of manhood. You men of forty and sixty, whose heads begin to be whitened with the frosts of age, does it not seem but yesterday since you gambolled with companions on the green and in the fields, and laughed and danced the hours away, from dewy morn till dusky eve! The impressions that remain of these early days are all but imperceptible. A name, a place, a countenance, rises up from amid the shadows of the past, but the years have glided from the vision as the clouds of the passing summer. And what of the years of riper age, in which hopes and fears, in alternate round, were born, and ripened, and died? Years in which love was plighted, and the household lighted up by the smiles of pure affection that have since been quenched in death. How little of all the gladsome or sombre experiences can you gather up from the tablet of memory? They have vanished and gone forever as the drops of dew in the morning sun, leaving behind them in too many cases the bitterness of memory and the anguish of despair. Some alas, can appropriate these sweet but touching lines of England's great humorist as they think of the past:

> " I remember, I remember
> The house where I was born,
> The little window where the sun
> Came peeping in at morn.
> He never came a wink too soon,
> Nor brought too long a day,
> But now I often wish the night
> Had borne my breath away!

> I remember, I remember
> The fir-trees dark and high,
> I used to think their tender tops
> Were close against the sky.
> It was a childish ignorance,
> But now 'tis little joy
> To know I'm further off from Heaven
> Than when I was a boy!"

Following up such a train of thought, we see the beauty and force of Scripture when speaking of the brevity and awful uncertainty of human existence. "For what is your life? It is even a vapour, that appeareth for a little time and then vanisheth away." How striking the illustration! As the mist or fog gradually and yet imperceptibly passes out of sight, so do we silently recede into the dark shadows of eternity. "My days are swifter than a post, they flee away, they see no good. They are passed away as the swift ships; as the eagle that hasteth to his prey. My days are swifter than a weaver's shuttle, and are spent without hope. O remember that my life is wind; mine eye shall no more see good." "Behold thou hast made my days as an handbreadth, and mine age is as nothing before Thee; verily every man, at his best estate, is altogether vanity." "Mine age is departed," says the good King Hezekiah, "and is removed from me as a shepherd's tent." "The days of our years are threescore and ten, and if by reason of strength they be fourscore years, yet is their strength labour and sorrow, for it is soon cut and we fly away." "All flesh is grass, and the glory thereof as the flower of the field." "We spend our years as a tale that is told." Human existence is thus compared to the frailest things in nature. The withering leaf, the fading flower, the vapour, the shadow, the shuttle. From the cradle to the grave is but a step!

The brevity of human life is surely then a fitting theme for meditation. It is the dictate of wisdom to number our days and apply our hearts to wisdom; to redeem the time, seeing that the days are evil. We may number our days and reap no profit by the exercise. It may be nothing more than a mere sentimental reverie, destitute of all manly resolution and decision' for the future. Merely to confess the shortness of our existence and bemoan our mortality, is a profitless employment for any immortal soul. To number our days by putting the question "How old art thou?" implies a right apprehension of the object of life—a determination honestly and zealously to discharge its duties, and to be always prepared for its close. Thus, and thus only, do we apply our hearts to · wisdom. That man is wise, according to the world's opinion, who in business matters is shrewd, and keen, and clever; who knows how to make a bargain; who can match and overreach his neighbor; who succeeds by unrighteousness and dishonest speculation, and wins the goal of popular applause. The patient, plodding, cautious, and honest merchant, who values conscience more than coin, and character more than capital, is stigmatized as stupid and ignorant, and altogether behind the age! But is it really so? Were there no eternity in prospect, were men mere animals, were annihilation our certain doom beyond the present, it might be wisdom for each man to gratify his sensual tastes. But is it so? Can it be so? Does any man believe it to be so? *After death comes the judgment*, is the united testimony of Scripture, Reason and Conscience —endless weal or woe. The question, then, "How old art thou?" in view of the terrible contingencies and awful realities of the future, is the most pressing and important question of the hour.

Some, perchance, who hear these words, have never seriously considered the possibility of an early and sudden death. They are conscious, notwithstanding, of many secret and open breaches of the law of God. It takes but a few years in life to become an expert in crime and skilled in wickedness—to sear the conscience and stain the comparative purity and innocence of childhood. Young in years, many are old in transgression. They have cherished evil thoughts, revelled in impure desires, and indulged in secret and open sin, which they would not for the world have revealed to their nearest and dearest friends. Does not the question "How old art thou?" bring up before the mind years of folly and shame that have passed to the bar of God with their dark and damning record? The name of God blasphemed—a Saviour despised—the Bible neglected—Sabbaths profaned—and the Sanctuary forsaken! Loving parents wept and prayed over you and wrestled for your salvation. On their bended knees they commended and committed you to the care of Heaven, and left the world with the glorious hope that with them you would share the unending felicities of Heaven! If not hardened beyond measure, such memories as these must flush the cheek and alarm the conscience. "How old art thou?" Old enough surely to retrace your steps. Old enough to know by sad experience that the way of the transgressor is hard, and that the steps of the profligate lead to perdition. Old enough to understand that the longer you delay, the more difficult, if not impossible, is a sincere repentance. *Old enough to die—to stand before the dread tribunal of judgment—to enter upon an eternity of remorse!* To reckon upon coming years is foolish. Death makes no compact with mortals, and grants to none a certain lease of life. The present moment is all that you possess—the rest is beyond your knowledge.

To others who read these lines, the question "How old art thou?" brings a certain measure of hopefulness as well as sadness. To such it may more appropriately be presented in its higher spiritual bearings, than as it relates to th eir term existence in the world. "How old are you in grace?" How long since you were born into the Kingdom of God's dear Son? Has the growth of piety in your soul steadily advanced in proportion to the years of your life? Have you reached any measure of maturity in faith, in knowledge, in patience, in joy and peace; and are these graces as evident to the world as they are sensible to your own experience? The stages of piety in your soul should keep pace with your earthly sojourn and the flight of time. As we draw near the end of life we should increase in strength and beauty of Christian character. What corresponding efforts, let me further ask, have you put forth, and what sacrifices have you made for the good of others? What results have God's afflictive dealings with you produced? Do you realize more and more, every day, that you are but a pilgrim and a stranger here—without home or possessions, exposed to danger and peril—and are you satisfied with this scene of change and trial until you find repose in that city which hath foundations whose maker and builder is God? It cannot be very long till the call shall come, and then farewell to sin and sorrow :

"Yet peace, my heart; and hush my tongue;
  Be calm, my troubled breast;
Each restless hour is hastening on
  The everlasting rest;
Thou knowest that the time thy God
  Appoints for thee is best."

The Builder and the Glory.

"**Even He shall build the Temple of the Lord, and He shall bear the Glory.**"—ZECHARIAH vi. 13.

The words of the text were intended to stimulate and encourage the Jews in the rebuilding of the temple. The captivity was now ended, and the exiles, returning to Jerusalem, found the temple in ruins; their holy and beautiful house was burned with fire. Many difficulties had to be encountered in the work of rebuilding. Their means were limited; they were comparatively few in number: their enemies persecuted them, and professed friends were lukewarm. The hearts of the people were therefore sorely discouraged, and but for the zeal and patriotism of a few noble-minded men, the work would never have been undertaken, far less completed. In these circumstances, Zechariah is sent to encourage them by promises and visions of success. In one of these visions which pass before him, he is commanded to take of the tribute-money which certain of the returned exiles had brought as a thank-offering, and make it into silver and golden crowns. These crowns he puts upon the head of the high priest Joshua, saying: "Thus speaketh the Lord of Hosts, saying, Behold the man whose name is the Branch; and He shall grow up out of His place and He shall build the temple of the Lord. Even He shall build the temple of the Lord, and He shall bear the glory." The prophecy, therefore, has a wider and remoter application and significance than the occasion when it was given. The person spoken of in these words as the builder of the temple, is neither Joshua nor Zerrubabel, though both of their names are mentioned in the context; but He of whom Joshua was but the type—the Lord Jesus Christ. The work described and the glory following can belong to no other. It thus very beautifully sets before us the progress of redemption, carried on through its different stages in the heart of individual believers, and in the church at large, until the final issue, when the Son of Man shall see of the travail of his soul, and shall be fully satisfied.

Frequently, in the Word of God, believers are likened to temples: "Know ye not that your body is the temple of the Holy Ghost, which is in you?" "The temple of God is holy, whose temple ye are!" The meaning of such language is evident. Temples are places consecrated and dedicated to the services of God—set apart for solemn worship—devoted not to secular or common-place transactions, but to communion with Jehovah. In the temple of old, glorious manifestations of the Deity were from time to time beheld. God dwelt in Zion. It was His rest. There He met His people and accepted their sacrifices of song and praise. Now in all these respects believers are temples. They are set apart for sacred uses—separated from the world to be a peculiar people, shewing forth the praise of Him who hath called them out of darkness into marvellous light. God's power and majesty are seen in every believer, as it can nowhere else be realized. The entire existence of such a man is to be devoted to God's service; his daily walk is to be with God, and his conversation to be in Heaven. In him God dwells by His spirit, shedding abroad His love—polishing his graces, adorning his character, and fitting him for the higher destiny and nobler employments of Heaven. Thus it may be said that individual believers are temples, and of every regenerated soul it may be said, "Christ shall bear the glory."

We prefer, however, to regard the temple spoken of as the Church of God in the world—not the visible, but the invisible Church. This Church is composed of all true believers, to whatever denomination they may belong, and the completed edifice, fresh from the great Builder's hand, shall soon stand forth, the admiration of the universe, even as the temple of old was the joy of all the earth. Then the corner-stone shall be laid with shoutings of "grace, grace unto it." Concerning this, the true Church of the living God, it is said, "He shall bear the glory."

In order to build a material structure, certain things are necessary:

First: A design must be prepared. The architect must first draw the requisite plans and specifications, including the probable cost of the materials, the method of their arrangement, and everything down to the most minute details.

Second: The materials must then be purchased— the wood and the stone, the silver and the gold, and all the fittings and furnishings necessary to conform to the design.

Third: These materials, once gathered, must be prepared. The stone must be hewn and polished, the wood sawn and carved, and the gold and silver fitted for their appropriate places.

Fourth: These materials, thus prepared, must be assigned their respective locations. The component parts, lying scattered on the ground, represent the essentials of the structure, but until the skilful hand unites them and puts them in their several relations, the confused mass reveals nothing of the architectural beauty and fair proportions of the design.

Fifth: Nor should we omit to mention that, in order to have a stable and permanent structure, there must be a good foundation. Without this all the previous toil and expenditure are in vain. The elements of nature, fitful and fickle, often lay n ruins the noblest specimens of architecture, and mock the pride and ingenuity of man.

Now, in all these respects it may be said, Christ builds the temple.

First: The design is His. From all eternity He planned the method, and filled up the details of the covenant of redemption. No mind but His was sufficient for this vast undertaking. He did not wait until man, helpless and fallen, stood aghast amid the ruins of Paradise, and then call upon the pure intelligences of heaven to undertake the work. No! Sitting amid the solitudes of Eternity, long ere man or seraphim existed, He contrived the glorious plan of Mercy, whereby depraved and guilty beings might be pardoned, and made living stones in the living temple, and this desolated and desecrated temple of humanity restored to more than its original grandeur.

Second: He purchased the materials. These were immortal souls, intended for the endless enjoyment of Heaven, but blighted and marred by the curse of sin. Earthly temples are built of material substances, in many cases rare, and precious, and costly; but what temple was ever built of material fit to be compared to living men? King David and King Solomon spared no expense in beautifying the temple of old. Cedar trees and palm trees from Lebanon—iron, silver and gold, and all manner of precious stones, were lavishly employed in its construction; but the cost of these were trifling, compared to the ransom paid for guilty man. The treasury of the Jewish commonwealth and the free-will offerings of the people supplied the necessary means to build the temple, but the blood of Jesus was poured out to purchase the material for this spiritual house. "Ye were not redeemed with corruptible things," says Peter, "as silver and gold, from your vain conversation received by tradition from your fathers, but with the precious blood of Christ, as a lamb without blemish and without spot." On no other terms was it possible that the purpose of Almighty love could be fulfilled, and this spiritual temple raised to the praise and honour of His grace.

Third: He prepares the materials. The marble fresh from the quarry, and the timber fresh from the forest, in their rude and unpolished normal state, were unfit to adorn the temple of old. Solomon, we are told, had all the materials fashioned and fitted for their appropriate places before the temple was begun. Then silently the workmen arranged these materials and built up the walls of the holy place. In like manner guilty souls are fitted and prepared for the spiritual temple. Thus to sanctify and cleanse a soul, and clothe it with all the necessary adornments that shall fit it to be an occupant of Heaven, is a far greater work than to create a world. This is what Christ is now doing by His spirit for His children. The iron in the veins of the earth is unfit, until smelted and moulded and hammered, for any one of the manifold uses to which it is applied. The gold and silver, that men dig for so eagerly, must be separated from the baser alloy and dust of earth 'ere they are fashioned into jewels or coronets, or pass current in men's hands as genuine coin. No more can human souls in their natural state enter Heaven. The Holy Spirit must purify them from uncleanness, and so refine their nature that the image of their Creator shall shine forth clear and radiant, unmistakably declaring their Divine origin in the past and their lofty destiny in the future. Many years were spent in building Solomon's temple, and a considerable period in erecting the second house of God. And so in like manner the work of renewing and fashioning human souls for the temple above is a slow and sometimes painful process. But however slow in some cases, its completion is certain. He that designed the plan of mercy and gave Himself for its accomplishment, will by His Spirit complete the work.

Fourth: He arranges and fits the materials for their appropriate places. "He builds the temple." Thus designed,—the materials purchased and prepared, nothing remains but that they be fitted into their appropriate places. In the temple of old there were degrees of external glory corresponding to different portions of the building. And so in the church upon earth and in the church of the redeemed, there are degrees of glory. All the saints are equally the subjects of renewing grace, and, in virtue of adoption, are the sons of God; but all are not equally gifted and endowed. To one is given pre-eminently the grace of faith; to another the grace of love; to another the grace of hope; and to another that of patience or meekness; to some there is given not one or two, but many graces, all in beauteous harmony. To one there is given a strong commanding intellect and mental endowments, fitted to mould other minds; to another is given self-denial, and a noiseless, blameless, unobtrusive life, that silently attracts our admiration by exhibiting the higher excellencies of Christian character. Now it is the work of the Chief Master Builder to arrange all these living stones in the framework of the spiritual temple. "They that be wise shall shine as the brightness of the firmament; and they that turn many to righteousness as the stars for ever and ever." Says St. Paul in writing to the Romans,—"Having gifts according to the grace that is given to us, whether prophecy, let us prophesy according to the proportion of faith, or ministry, let us wait on our ministry; he that teacheth on teaching, and he that exhorteth on exhortation." And writing to the

Ephesians, he says, "Unto every one of us is given grace according to the measure of the gift of Christ. He gave some apostles and some prophets, and some evangelists and some pastors and teachers, for the perfecting of the saints, for the work of the ministry, for the edifying of the body of Christ." What do such passages mean, but that as in the resurrection the spiritual bodies shall differ one from the other—as one star differeth from another in glory, so also shall it be in regard to the redeemed in the temple above. As in the church below, believers occupy the places assigned them by the master of assemblies, so in the completed spiritual temple, according to the measure and perfection of our graces shall be our position and our honour.

Fifth: And finally, I need only add that the builder of the temple is at the same time its foundation. "Ye are built upon the foundation of the apostles and prophets, Jesus Christ Himself being the chief corner-stone, in whom all the building, fitly framed together, groweth unto an holy temple in the Lord." As Christ is at once high priest and sacrifice, so is He the author and finisher of the Christian's spiritual being. Great is the mystery of godliness! This foundation is a sure one—tried and tested, firm and stable, "Behold," says the prophet, "I lay in Zion, for a foundation, a stone; a, tried stone—a precious stone—a sure foundation; he that believeth shall not make haste." Says the Psalmist, "The stone which the builders refused is become the head of the corner." Upon this foundation God is now building His spiritual temple. On this rock of ages His saints can rest in perfect peace. The foundation of God standeth sure—the Lord knoweth them that are His. Well, then, may the Christian sing in reference to the certainty of his salvation :—

> "How firm a foundation, ye saints of the Lord,
> Is laid for your faith in His excellent word;
> What more can He say than to you He hath said,
> You who unto Jesus for refuge have fled.

The glory of this completed temple rightly belongs to Christ. "He shall bear the glory." The names of those who have designed such edifices as St. Peter's, in Rome, St. Paul's and Westminster Abbey, in London, are imperishable. No one needs to write a history of their genius. We have only to look around and above us, as we stand under these mighty cathedral domes, in order to judge of their greatness. So we have but to study the plan and work of redemption in its merest outlines in order to perceive the perfection and grandeur of the achievement. Just think—

First: Of the materials out of which the building has been framed. Not polished stones ready for the builder's use, but rude, unshapely blocks, demanding the skill of the Infinite mind to fit them for their place. Out of the ruins of creation, from the most degraded and abandoned of our race, are these living stones selected for the spiritual temple.

Second: Consider next the perfection of the building, though constructed out of such crude material. Scarcely any humanly constructed edifice is perfect. The skilful eye will detect some flaw or defect—something that is capable of improvement and of greater beauty. But not so with this spiritual temple. It is complete in all its parts—every separate stone is necessary; to add or detract would but destroy the beauty of the entire structure.

Third: Consider once more the difficulties to be overcome in erecting this temple. The difficulties were great which confronted Nehemiah and the Israelites at the building of the second temple, when open hostility and secret conspiracies endeavored to delay the accomplishment of the work. But greater far were the obstacles opposed to the building of the spiritual temple. The principalities and powers of earth have been and still are the enemies of Christ and His church. However Satan's kingdom may be divided on minor points, his servants are as one on this, that Messiah's kingdom must not prevail. But in spite of all opposition it advances. Nothing is too hard for the Captain of our Salvation. Conqueror over death and the grave, He shall subdue all His enemies, and raise this temple upon the ruins of His foes. Delays and pauses may appear in the work, but at the appointed time the building shall be completed, amid the rejoicing hallelujahs of the redeemed. Then shall the song of triumph be heard "the kingdoms of this world have become the kingdoms of our God and His Christ, and He shall reign for ever." The glory accruing from this work must be infinite, imperishable as the temple itself—lasting as the heavens. To God in Christ, and God alone, belongs the praise of salvation from first to last, and this He shall receive from all parts of the visible creation, from all ranks of intelligent beings, from the Church below and the Church above.

More particularly we remark, He bears the glory, inasmuch as He is—(a). Glorified by the Father and the Holy Spirit. These Divine persons glorified Him upon the earth, when engaged in the actual work of redemption. Again and again they testified their approbation of His sufferings, a voice from the opened heavens saying, " This is my beloved Son, in whom I am well pleased." Had it not been for the approval of heaven, Christ would never have entered upon or completed the work. It was theirs as much as His, though he was the agent delegated to perform it: And that this work, when completed upon earth, was accepted by the Father, is abundantly proved by the royal honours on which the Saviour entered at his death. "When He had purged away our sins" He was received to the Father's right hand, highly exalted above all principalities and powers, and might and dominion, and every name that is named, not only in this world but in that which is to come. There, now, He sits clothed with sovereignty, and wielding the sceptre of universal empire. (b). He is glorified by the angelic hosts. The angels, while they cannot fully grasp the wondrous mystery of redemption, are lost in amazement as they gaze upon it, and yield Him the homage of their hearts. Over this glorious achievement the morning stars sang together, and all the sons of God shouted for joy. They cast their crowns before His feet; they acknowledge Him as their Lord; they cheerfully execute His mandates; they fly hither and thither on works of mercy or judgment; they hover round the bedside of the dying saint, and bear the spirit upward to the celestial world, that the anthem of redemption may have another singer and the swell of praise be louder. In circling bands around the throne they cry out, "Worthy is the Lamb that was slain to receive power and riches, and wisdom, and strength, and honour, and glory, and blessing."

(c). He is glorified in the ministrations of the sanctuary. Christ and His salvation is here the constant, unvarying theme. Nowhere does the glory of Emmanuel shine forth so resplendently as in the congregation of His saints, when they meet to pray and praise, to engage in solemn acts of communion, to read and meditate, and behold the shinings of His face. The great end of the ministry is to save souls, and every soul converted is another star in the crown of Jesus. (d). He is glorified in the person of His saints on earth. "They shall hang upon Him," says the Prophet, "all the glory of His Father's house." They glorify Him in the simple act of faith, when they mould their character and order their conversation after His example, when they walk in His footsteps and are conformed to His image; they glorify Him in the fires of persecution, by patiently enduring those trials. and chastisements which are necessary to sanctification, and which are the precursors of coming glory. (e). Finally, He is glorified now, and shall be still further glorified, by the redeemed in heaven. The work of saints in the temple above is unceasing praise. "Thou wast slain and hast redeemed us to God by Thy blood, out of every kindred and tongue and people and nation. Salvation to our God which sitteth upon the throne, and unto the Lamb." "I heard a voice from heaven as the voice of many waters and as the voice of a great thunder; and I heard the voice of harpers harping with their harps, and they sung as it were a new song before the throne and before the four beasts and the elders, and no man could learn that song but the hundred-and forty-four thousand which were redeemed from the earth." All this adoration is directed toward Christ. It it Jesus' name that sounds so sweetly upon their harps. It is Jesus and His love which fills their hearts and trembles upon their lips. It is Jesus' presence that gladdens their spirits and inspires their song. Such praise and adoration is sincere. They know the value of redemption, they feel their indebtedness to sovereign love. Their united praises give evidence of the comprehensiveness of salvation, for they are gathered out of all peoples and kindreds and tongues. Living far apart and in different ages of the world, they have all been united in one and in Christ, through the atoning sacrifice of Calvary.

He shall bear the glory. The prediction cannot be fully realized until the present dispensation ends. Now the glory radiates from different points, then it shall be concentrated in heaven. The temple is yet building. Many stones are yet unhewn and unpolished. Darkness and superstition still cover the fairest portion of the earth. Idolatrous shrines and Hindoo temples are yet crowded by worshippers of unknown gods ; Paganism holds millions in slavery, and smears countless altars with human blood and human sacrifices. The time has not yet arrived when there shall be but one temple and one altar in the world; one Mediator, one High Priest and Intercessor, adored and worshipped as the rightful possessor of earth and heaven. But the time is drawing near. He *shall* bear the glory. "Thy people shall be willing in the day of Thy power."

> "Jesus shall reign where'er the sun
> Does his successive journeys run,
> His kingdom stretch from shore to shore,
> Till moons shall wax and wane no more.
>
> "For Him shall endless prayers be made,
> And endless blessings crown His head;
> His name like sweet perfume shall rise
> With every morning sacrifice."

The glory thus completed shall be continuous throughout eternity. The gems upon Messiah's crown shall never fade nor lose their lustre. Every new discovery made by the Saints in Heaven shall but increase their joy and call forth greater outbursts of praise. They never shall become weary, of adoring the name of Jesus, or giving Him that honour which is rightly His. Eternity shall seem all too short, and the sanctified soul too feeble to exhaust the wonders of redemption.

> "Angels and men may strive to raise
> Harmonious their adoring songs;
> But who can fully speak His praise,
> From human or angelic tongues!"

"The Wasting of the Outward, and the Renewal of the Inner Man."

"**Though** our outward man perish, yet the inward man is renewed day by day."—2ND COR. iv. 16.

No man can imagine what pressure of calamity his human nature can endure. When we look back over a lengthened existence, scarred and beaten by the storms of affliction, the thought uppermost in the mind is, How has this poor frail mortal tenement stood so long? If the sad scroll of lamentation and woe had been spread out before our eyes in the bright days of youth, we should have fainted at the prospect. The strongest faith would have been shaken, and our hearts left to the horrors of despair. It is a wonderful instance of God's knowledge of the feebleness of the creature, and His desire to make our trials endurable, that they are to us unknown—that Providence hides from our gaze the unexpected evils of the coming day, and the accumulated sorrows of our lives, and that as these trials come there are alleviations, supports and consolations, that enable us to bear them beyond our most sanguine expectations.

These words declare the perishable and destructible nature of the outward tabernacle under repeated strokes. That it continues so long is indeed marvellous, when we take into account the sickness, the dangers, and the constant troubles to which it is exposed. We feel on reflection the truth of the poet's words, when, speaking of the brevity and uncertainty of existence, he says:—

> "Our life contains a thousand strings,
> And dies if one be gone.
> Strange! that a harp of thousand strings,
> Should keep in tune so long."

Some are smitten to the earth at once, and wither under the blast of God's afflictive providences, as the leaf dries up under the scorching heat of the summer's sun. But as a general rule our trials come so gradually that for many years the body continues to discharge its normal functions, although impaired and weakened. There is a gradual wasting and deteriorating—a pulling down process, going on in every human frame; in some more rapidly than in others; but in all more or less discernible! The longest life is after all but a funeral march to the grave, and the strongest frame ultimately bends to the decree of Nature. Nay, it would seem in many cases as if special and increasing trials were sent for the purpose of shortening the already brief and limited span of human existence.

Paul felt this breaking up in his physical constitution when he penned these words. No man was ever so lacerated and scourged as he, and the character of his sufferings were just of that kind fitted to wear out the strongest systems. Shipwreck, perils, weariness, painfulnesss, watchings, fastings, hunger and thirst, cold and nakedness, dark and loathsome dungeons and excruciating tortures, these were the daily experiences of the apostle's life. His immense energy of nature, his strong impulses and dominant will, doubtless served for a time to carry him over such persecutions, with little tangible evidences of their effects. But, by-and-bye, he felt that Paul the aged was a very different man even from Paul in the prime of manhood, and when starting in the Christian life. The very sap of his body was drying up, the elements of his physical strength were wasting away, and very soon, if continued upon earth, he might be unfitted for the more arduous cares and labours of the ministry. But if so, no word of complaint or regret escapes his lips. So long as he can work for God he intends to be active in the campaign. He is determined that nothing but absolute necessity shall force him into retirement. Nay, more, he finds cause for gratitude and joy in the very fact that his infirmity and weakness ensure him supernatural mental vigour. If his brow be furrowed with care, and his whole outer man be enfeebled by age and suffering, he has more than a compensation in the energy and buoyancy of his spiritual powers. "Though the outer man perisheth," or is wasting away, says the apostle, "the inner man is renewed day by day."

The inward man is evidently the spiritual being —the soul—that which constitutes the real man— that which shapes the conduct and moulds the destiny of the future. It is independent of the body, unless in so far as the body is its dwellingplace, and provides it with suitable instruments for its earthly existence. Nay, from analogy, we reasonably conclude that the soul, unencumbered by the body, shall be able to reach far higher results and follow out the ends of its existence in far more favourable circumstances than in its present state of being. The glorified body, perfectly adapted to the sanctified spirit, and unaffected by those outward changes that in the present life enfeeble it, shall rather aid than hinder its progress in searchings after Divine truth. "Now we see through a glass darkly"—because our spiritual vision is dim and cloudy by reason of the soul's connection with the body—"but then we shall see face to face. Now we know in part, but then we shall know even as also we are known."

Leaving all speculation for the present aside, let us meditate for a little on the truth contained in these words—the renewal or strengthening of the inner man in proportion to the perishing or wasting of the outer.

First: The language implies that the Divine life has already been implanted in the soul. It is not a *creation* that is spoken of, but rather the *increase* or development of what already exists. At conversion a new principle takes possession of the soul, hitherto unknown. It is called regeneration—the new birth or the new creation;—language in either and every case implying the thoroughness of the change. It is the calling into existence of a character and condition which had no being before. There are new feelings and desires—new aims—not complete estrangement from sin, but strong inclinations after holiness—a leaving behind the things of the present and a seeking after those of the future —a complete surrender of all that the person *is* or *has* to the service of God. The necessity of such a change in the natural man, and the fact that such a change takes place in every Christian, no one denies; but how it takes place, and when, varies in the experience of different individuals. Sometimes the change is almost imperceptible. The seeds of holiness, sown in early life, germinate and strengthen without any violent emotions being experienced. This is more especially the case with the children of God-fearing, pious parents, who often pass on from stage to stage of their religious experience without any conscious radical change in feeling or in life. But at other times the crisis of conversion is distinctly marked, by terrible throes and bitter pangs. Doubt, disbelief, horrid anticipations of Divine judgment, and the stinging accusations of a guilty conscience, precede the coming in of peace and assured hope. Darkness the most profound, and despair the most bewildering, possess the soul before light and joy find entrance. Sometimes, again, conversion is experienced in early years. We dare not limit the spirit's operations on the heart of even the youngest child. Grace can as savingly bring to Jesus the Sabbath-school scholar as the aged and infirm sinner. Nay, in the former case the sincerity of the change is more likely, and steady continuance in the faith more hopeful and lasting. In other cases, conversion does not take place until manhood or womanhood has been reached; and only after a long period of reflection, and after a most searching investigation of the truths and blessings of Christianity, as superior to all other systems of religion. Indeed, it is quite possible for a man to be a real child of God, and for a time be unconscious of the change. The crisis may be past, while the fever remains, not entirely subdued. Wrong ideas in regard to what the change carries with it often prevent the believer from enjoying all the comfort and satisfaction that are rightly his because he is already Christ's. But by whatever means brought about, the change is vital. It is a passing from death into life, from sleep to active consciousness, from darkness to light, from Satan to God. It is the casting out of all vain imaginations, and the indwelling of the spirit of God, whereby the believing heart becomes a temple of the Holy Ghost. It is this that the Apostle speaks of in the text as the inner man, and elsewhere—" If any man be in Christ he is a new creature; old things are passed away; behold all things are become new."

Second: This Divine life, or the inner man, is renewed day by day. Says the prophet Isaiah—" They that wait upon the Lord shall renew their strength; they shall mount up with wings as eagles; they shall run and not be weary, and they shall walk and not faint." "The path of the just," says Solomon, "is as the shining light, shining more and more unto the perfect day." "They go from strength to strength," (unwearied) says the Psalmist; "every one of them in Zion appeareth before God." And in the 103rd Psalm, David speaks of Christian vigour as being renewed like the eagles. The process of spiritual development is gradual, but ever onward. The renewed soul is dependent every moment of its earthly existence upon the power of Jehovah. Its advancement, its continued and increasing growth, is due to the agency of the Holy Spirit. Just as completely as the body depends upon the bounty of God for its continued support, does the spiritual part of our nature rely upon sovereign grace. Conversion is a miracle, and continuance and advancement in holiness is equally a miracle, due to nothing in the man himself. The language implies that wherever conversion is real there will be constant progress. There may be what seem repulses in the Christian life—periods of rest and inactivity in comparison with the more eager and earnest moments subsequent to conversion—but during the entire period of the Christian's earthly existence there is constant renewal, a polishing and perfecting of the graces of the spirit, a reaching forth to that holiness "without which no man can see the Lord." This does not conflict in the least with the melancholy record of God's people, who mourn over coldness in the Divine life, and who rather seem to be losing ground than achieving conquests. After a certain age, and as the body approaches maturity, the changes that occur are less easily recognized. So in spiritual experience, after the first years of enthusiasm, and burning zeal, and love, there follows a calmness—a composure—a fixedness of belief and serenity of mind, that may be mistaken for retrogression rather than advancement. The Christian's standard of holiness is daily becoming more difficult of attainment—his distance from Christ appears to himself to be greater, though absolutely far less than it was months or years before. His attainments in the Divine life are so meagre, and his plans and purposes so far in excess of his actual performances, that he hastily concludes that spiritual life is declining. This is by no means the universal experience of God's people. There are many who can testify to progress—who can contrast the present with the past, and gratefully acknowledge God's goodness in their ripeness for heaven and their love of religious ordinances. Their progress, though not perhaps greater than in the cases mentioned formerly, is more palpable to the eye of faith, and produces more hopeful and joyous emotions. But in every case, whether perceived or unperceived —whether greater or less—*there is progress*. It must be so where there is spiritual life. In God's family there are no still-born children, and no cases of fatal decline. There are the stronger and the weaker, the more rugged and the more delicate, the more heroic and the more sensitive, but all without exception grown in grace and in the knowledge of the Lord Jesus Christ.

Third: The words still further imply that the renewal of the inner man is in proportion to the decay or wasting of the outer; and it seems to be implied that, without this decay and wasting, no very exalted standard of Christian life can be attained. The afflictions of the body, the Apostle seems to argue, are medicine for the soul. Sleepless nights, feverish brows and quick-throbbing pulses, are, under the Spirit's guidance, real means of grace. As the flesh gets weaker the soul becomes stronger; as life's material enjoyments become fewer, Heaven's promises become sweeter; as the natural eye fades the spiritual brightens; as the ear becomes closed to the melody of earth it becomes more acute to hear the music of the redeemed. The bed of affliction and the darkened chamber become meeting-places for God and the soul, where sweetest communion and richest anticipations of the land of Beulah are enjoyed. Such is the promise of the 92nd Psalm; "They shall bring forth fruit in old age," which is equally true of the hoary-headed saint as of the young believer in life's closing moments. The richest and ripest clusters of grace are then gathered. Afflictions, like the warm sunbeams, ripen, mellow and mature Christian character, call forth into view unseen elements and precious qualities hitherto unknown, until at last the grain is fit to be garnered in the heavenly storehouse. An apple tree in blossom is beautiful to behold; but who mourns the absence of the blossoms when they are succeeded by the rich and luscious fruit? And who should regret the decay of the body when we are assured that it precedes the completely sanctified soul? What we call untimely deaths in the case of God's children are the reverse. Is it ever untimely to go to heaven? Is it ever untimely to enter upon the immortal youth of paradise? When men suddenly and unexpectedly fall heirs to massive fortunes, do we speak of it as an untimely calamity? No, we rejoice, and congratulate them upon their elevation from poverty to riches; and when God calls His suffering saints to heaven, to the enjoyment of eternal riches and unfading joys, shall we persist in speaking of untimely deaths? No, rather let us regard such deaths as the call of the beloved to the bride, as the grasping of the crown and the wreathing of the laurel. I am sure that some here can testify to the wonderful renewal of spiritual strength they have often witnessed when standing round the deathbeds of God's saints. Faltering tongues have eloquently discoursed of Jesus' love; trembling hands have firmly clasped the cross with exulting joy; "Countenances overspread with the pallor of death, have been lighted up with the radiance of heaven; and the loftiest ascriptions of praise have been uttered by voices already feeble and indistinct with approaching dissolution. In the Valley of the Shadow of Death the Holy Ghost has put the final and completing touches to the image of Christ; the last remains of sin have seemed to die out, and heaven itself to have come down to earth!"

To friends, there is something sad in marking the gradual decline of health, and the sapping of the foundations of natural strength in the beloved son or daughter. To the suffering saint it is often very hard to bear. We naturally all shrink from pain and sorrow. Death makes cowards of us all. There are also other ingredients in a lingering sickness that intensify the anguish of the body. To an active mind, accustomed to constant exercise in the cause of Christ, how wearisome at first is compulsory absence from the house of God—from the table of the Lord—from the little class in the Sabbath school! These in former days have been the indirect sources of the Christian's strength, but now he must draw directly from the fountain-head—he must be taught experimentally that God's presence is not confined to earthly temples, and that graces can sometimes grow equally well, nay better, in the shade than in the sunshine. And how does the flesh at first rebel, when for months, or it may be years, existence is confined to the one little chamber—and yet God makes that condition of seeming uselessness and inactivity glorious in results to friends and acquaintances who from time to time stand round the dying couch. The last thing that the believer learns in this world is that God can be equally served and His cause advanced by silence as by speech; by sitting at His feet as by serving at the table; by patient resignation to His will as by daily conflict in the world. As John Milton says,—

> " God doth not need
> Either man's work or His own gifts; who best
> Bear His mild yoke, they serve Him best. His state
> Is kingly; thousands at His bidding speed,
> And post o'er land and ocean without rest—
> *They also serve who only stand and wait.*"

You and I may soon lie on such weary beds of suffering as I have been describing. What, let me ask, shall enable us to endure—to bear the chastising rod of our Heavenly Father with resignation and contentment? Not our natural powers, not any strength of resolution that we may then possess—Death makes the stoutest heart to tremble, and blanches the proudest cheek. The Apostle tells us how we may be victorious over death and suffering. "For which cause we faint not," he says, referring evidently to the statement of the context, that believers shall be raised up with the Lord Jesus, and presented blameless on the day of judgment. All things are for their sakes—whether Paul or Apollos, or Cephas or the world, or things present or things to come—because they are Christ's, and Christ is God's. It is this knowledge as a personal experience that keeps from fainting or sinking in the hour of conflict with the prince of darkness. All our mortal strength is unequal to the last encounter with Death. Nothing but the omnipotent arm of Jehovah and the presence of the Holy Spirit can make us conquerors. The blood of Christ extracts the sting from Death, and gives us victory over the grave!

Children in the Market-Place.

"But whereunto shall I liken this generation? It is like unto children sitting in the market, and calling unto their fellows, and saying, We have piped unto you and ye have not danced; we have mourned unto you and ye have not lamented."—MATT. xi. 16, 17.

A man upon a sick-bed frequently possesses a peculiar taste. What in reality is sweet seems bitter, and what is pleasant appears sour; what in his ordinary health and vigor is most relished, is rejected and regarded with intense feelings of disgust. The taste is not only peculiar, but exceedingly changeable. To-day he fancies that a certain article of food would please and satisfy the palate, but no sooner is it presented than he loathes it, and craves for another change. The strongest affection often fails to meet all the whimsical demands of the diseased constitution, and the most enduring and patient temperament often becomes wearied under such long and repeated irritations. Such a condition of mind and body is, of course, abnormal. It is due to the existence of some malady which, for the time being, changes the disposition, and to some extent confuses the mind. Once the disease is removed, and the patient restored to health, the normal taste returns, and the common articles of diet are more than sufficient to satisfy the keenest appetite.

In later years the subject of "colour-blindness" has attracted much notice, and agitated scientific circles very largely. This disease, if such it can be called, consists in a certain defect of vision, whereby certain colours are not distinguishable, or colours are alike invisible as such. Most people see seven colours in the rainbow; but people who suffer from colour-blindness see only two. Dalton, the celebrated scientific discoverer, was himself defective in vision. He saw only two colours, yellow and blue, or at the most, three, yellow, blue and purple. To his eye there was no difference between red and green; and when asked by Professor Whewell to what he would compare his scarlet gown, pointed to the leaves of the trees around him. Dugald Stewart, also, the great metaphysician, was affected with this same colour-blindness. He could not distinguish a crimson fruit, like the Siberian crab, from the leaves of the tree on which it grew, otherwise than by its difference of form. Investigations as to the cause of this singular defect in the vision show that often it is hereditary, and that it does not arise purely from disease of the eye, but from some peculiar condition of the brain or sensorium. The cause seems to be somewhere between the eye, as an organ of perception, and the mind—the latter being incapacitated to perceive the difference of colours. What has all this to do with the text, you will be ready to ask? Much every way, I answer. There are hundreds of men and women who, in regard to religion, are just as fickle and whimsical and unreasonable as the sick man, whose taste is so capricious and difficult to please. They are continually seeking after novelties in matters of doctrine and in forms of worship. They have some serious fault to find with every sect and denomination of Christians. They have no fixed religious home; they profit by no preacher, and are benefitted by no Church organization. Like the people who are afflicted with colour-blindness, they are morally and spiritually incapacitated to perceive the truth or grasp it. Truth seems to their conception error, and error truth. What to others seems beautiful and comely in the ordinances of the sanctuary, appears to them distasteful and disgusting. What profits and nourishes sincere and candid minds, who wait upon the ministrations of the Gospel, and receive the word with meekness and humility, leaves upon their minds no impressions whatever, other than a still stronger opposition to the truth. The Church is a fraud; religion is all hypocrisy; creeds and confessions are hollow and worthless forms; members of churches are uncharitable and despotic censors, and ministers, as a class, conceited and self-righteous knaves. Now, bad as is the human heart, there is something abnormal where such feelings exist, and where such language is spoken. I know some men speak so who do not think so; but others, I am willing to believe, speak so because they thus conscientiously believe. It is such persons I am now speaking of, and what I assert is, that as a class they are the victims of colour-blindness—they do not look the truth fairly in the face; they are unable to separate the false and the real—they suffer from moral obliquity, or, to use the language of Scripture, "the god of this world hath blinded their minds, lest the light of the glorious Gospel of Christ should shine unto them."

Such persons are peculiar to no one period of the world's history. Since the creation of Adam on to the present moment, there have been people deformed in body, pale and sickly in their physical constitution, and defective in vision. And since the organization of the Church in the world, there have been quite as many who suffer under mental maladies, rendering them constant fault-finders and grumblers. Such there were in the days of Christ, as we learn from our text. They were neither pleased with the Old Testament dispensation nor the New. They found fault alike with prophets and apostles; with John the Baptist and with Jesus Christ. They were wayward, ill-natured, capricious, discontented, like ill-humoured children, whom it is impossible to please in any way. One portion desired this, and another portion that; what pleased the one displeased the other,—so that no form of doctrine and no description of religious life could be devised, suited to their whimsical tastes. The grand evil lay in the fact, that they did not really know what they did want. They enjoyed a certain satisfaction in censuring every new teacher that claimed their attention, and in abusing all who did not coincide with their groundless objections.

I take this to be the general truth contained in the text. Says Christ, "But whereunto shall I liken this generation? It is like unto children sitting in the markets and calling unto their fellows—their companions—and saying, We have piped unto you and ye have not danced; we have mourned and ye have not lamented." It was universal dissatisfaction all round. Some of the group wished to play at a mock marriage, but the others from some cause not mentioned refused to join them. Hence discontent and vexation on the part of those who desired their playmates to join in the dance, or simulate the mourning. The last named portion of the group preferred something else, which displeased the others, and so there existed nothing but ill-will, mutual crimination and recrimination—an atmosphere of complaint and discontent. This, says Christ, is the character of the Jews of my day.

You remind me of a band of giddy, thoughtless, unreasonable children—at one time gay, and at another time grave. You expect that everyone should conform to your likes and dislikes—your passions and prejudices. You abuse all others who will not court your favour or agree with your erroneous views and sinful practices. You are displeased with John the Baptist because of his rigid, austere life and urgent calls to repentance; because he would not prophesy smooth things, and accommodate his teaching to meet the depraved tastes of the age; because, in a word, he would not dance to your piping. You are equally displeased with my teaching and conduct, although in many respects it differs materially from that of John. Because I exhibit religion as a life of cheerfulness, of activity and love for the erring and sinful; because I will not weep to your dirge and countenance your hypocrisy, I am denounced and branded as a man of impure life and a propagator of false doctrine. John rebuked you for your licentiousness; I censure you for your self-righteousness, but neither of us suit your tastes—you condemn alike our persons and reject our counsels.

The Jews had strong objections to Christ's doctrine, as well as His morality. He preached and offered a salvation free to all who would accept it, having no favourite in any one nation or in any one class of society,—as intended for guilty men, everywhere, whether Jew or Gentile. This to the narrow-minded Jew was most unpalatable doctrine Only to the seed of Abraham did the Jew desire the blessings of salvation to extend. The national creed was exclusive, the Church was exclusive, and the Jew would have heaven exclusive also. Then again, Christ taught the utter worthlessness of all good works, to secure in part or in whole the favour of God—a doctrine which to self-righteous Pharisees was peculiarly hard to accept. It seemed unreasonable that acts of benevolence and a pure unblemished moral character should not receive some consideration and compensation in the sight of God. If the drunkard and the profligate had an equal chance of heaven, through the mercy of God, with the man who fasted and prayed and did penance, then what inducement was there to strive after an outwardly moral and virtuous character. The daily practice of Christ, too, in society, was as strange and inconsistent with their views of decorum as was His teaching. He was eminently social and familiar with the lower classes of the nation. He met and conversed with men in the ordinary walks of life—nay, He was oftener found in the houses and at the tables of the poor, than at the feasts and banquets of the rich and honourable. He laid aside the severe asceticism that seemed to characterize the Baptist, and, instead of dwelling in the desert and living on locusts and wild honey, He entered into all the innocent enjoyments that came in his way. Publicans and sinners, like Zaccheus,—Mary Magdalene, out of whom seven devils had been cast,—outcasts and reprobates of the deepest dye, were among His companions and friends.. At the marriage of Cana of Galilee He was present, a cheerful spectator of the innocent festivity and enjoyment of the hour, and in the house of Simon the leper, He was also found a not less welcome guest. He mingled with the utmost freedom in every topic of discussion, and became all things to all men, if thereby they might be saved. Now, such conduct, so different from the Scribes and Rabbis, the Jews could not understand. The

Pharisees especially, who kept themselves rigidly apart from all who did not come up to the standard of ceremonial sanctity, denounced the Saviour as a glutton and a wine-bibber—as a man who loved pleasure and fleshly lusts—a man of impure and dishonest principles. It is very true such a charge could not by any possibility be brought against John the Baptist, and yet equally with Christ he found no favour in their eyes. John neither sat with them nor drank with them; he never entered into familiar conversation, either in the market-place or at their tables. He kept himself studiously aloof from all contact with the men of his day, living like a lonely hermit in his wilderness cell; but such conduct was as vehemently vilified as that of Christ. "He was possessed of a devil;"—his reserved and melancholy temperament was due to diabolic agency; he was a poor crazed fanatic, altogether unworthy of their confidence or respect. Thus it happened that, whatever phase of religious life was presented—no matter how dissimilar and extreme—suffered alike the most unjust aspersions. The sympathy of Christ and the austerity of John were alike blameable in the eyes of men who were determined to find fault with every appeal to the conscience, and every personal application to the life.

Now it is not difficult to find such people at the present day, and that even within the pale of the visible Church—not, it may be, *members* of any Church —but hearers of the Gospel. They are not infidels— far from it. They will stoutly maintain the integrity and inspiration of the Scriptures against all attacks of sceptics. They are not immoral or licentious in their lives—far from it. Like the Pharisees of old, their standard of moral purity is high. None are so severe upon the smallest defection from virtue—none are so ready to denounce the current opinion that the common vices of the age are but venial sins. Nor can it be said that they are careless in their Church attendance, or indifferent to the claims of the Sabbath, and the value of a day of rest. With wonderful regularity they attend some place of worship on the Lord's day, and go through the forms of devotion with apparent sincerity. Nor are they so liberal in their views as to say that all forms of religion, whether Popish, Puseyite, or Protestant, are equally good; but somehow or other their religious life is a series of negations—without anything commendable or really useful to the world at large. They lead an unsettled, migratory life, from creed to creed, and Church to Church. Like the dove that was sent out of the ark ere the waters had subsided, they find no rest or satisfaction in any existing Church organization. They long for apostolic simplicity and apostolic purity—for a state of things that can never be obtained in the present condition of our race—a state which, even were it realized, would fail to meet the wants of such censorious and captious critics.

It is a most unenviable state of mind that we are describing, and the man is to be pitied who possesses it. There surely are, at the present day, variety enough of denominations to meet the most singular tastes. Surely some church organization may be found where every man who desires to labour for the Master may find scope enough for the healthy exercise of all his powers, and for personal advancement in the Divine life. Perfect purity in worship, in creed, or in discipline, is not to be expected in the visible Church; but is there not perfection enough to satisfy all but the most unreasonable of mortals? Surely it argues something wrong in the moral sense when a man spends his lifetime in searching out defects either in the individual professors of religion or the Church in its collective capacity. And yet how frequently we meet with or hear of such! They see nothing but the evil of whatever is presented to them. They have a natural attraction for what is defective; fault-finding and ill-natured criticism is their forte. They seem to regard such a faculty of fault-finding as a special gift, for the due cultivation and exercise of which they are responsible. What is good in Christian character, and commendable in Christian Churches, entirely escapes their notice. What is defective and unlovely is eagerly seized upon and magnified to the lasting injury of the cause of truth.

Now it may be said truly that if the perfect innocence of Christ's character, and the pure principles of Christianity, which He published to the world, failed to satisfy all who were brought under their influence, it is not marvellous though the much less perfect character of modern Christians, and the much less complete presentation of the truth from our modern pulpits, should find a similar reception. But we are anxious to find out what are the specific objections that such a class of persons prefer against the Church of Christ, and to endeavour to remove these objections by showing their unreasonableness. Is it that in the visible church there are so many incomplete, or, if you will, inconsistent Christians— persons whose conduct, in your estimation, is at variance with the faith they profess to believe and practise? If such is the ground of objection, its removal is impossible in the present condition of the Church. A Christian is by no means a perfect man, either at conversion or at any other period of his subsequent life. We are not to look upon a professor of religion as a marble statue when it comes from the artist's hands, complete and ready for criticism in the exhibition room, defying the most minute investigation, and calling on the outside world to see what a saint he has become. So far from this, Christians, for the most part, are but entrants in the school of Christ, beginners in learning, and practising the elements of Divine morality—full of incongruities and anomalies, which only time, and the grace of God, can remove and cancel. A man should join himself to the Church of Christ not simply that he may the better expend his energies for the good of humanity, but that he may personally be helped and assisted in the midst of weakness and temptation. For a man to object to the Church of Christ because it contains many erring and fallible brethren, is to proceed upon an entire misconception of what the Church really is, and what it was intended to accomplish when placed in the world by its Divine Head. Before a man refuses to connect himself with some one of the evangelical churches of the present day, he should object, not on the grounds of imperfect memhership, but that none are to be found within its pale possessed of his own holiness and unexceptional morality. Such a man certainly, when found, deserves translation to the Church triumphant, that his garments may not be soiled through contact with the infirmities and weakness of the Church on earth! Or, is it because the discipline and government of the Christian Church, is not what you think the Scriptures teach, that you still stand without? Well then, what system of government do you prefer? At the present day where there are so many denominations, and such endless variety of church order, from the hierarchy of the Pope, down to the latest democracy, surely there must be some form that meets your views. No church pretends to have its discipline and government perfect, unless it be the Church of Rome. The New Testament Scriptures with the exception of certain cardinal principles which lie at the root of all well ordered government, gives but little help in the department of ecclesiastical order, and leaves it very much to each denomination to form its own code of laws, according as it thinks them most in accordance with the Spirit of the New Testament. But are forms of government and methods of discipline so vital and important that a man is justified to refuse the association and fellowship of believers, because to his mind there is some defect! Surely not. Suggest improvements—let your voice be heard in support of them; give the church the benefit of your larger experience, but do not in your fault-finding spirit seek to detract from her present usefulness, or refuse your wise co-operation. Or is it the mode in which truth is presented at the present day, that creates your opposition to existing church organizations? It cannot be the truth itself, for the Gospel as preached by Christ and his apostles, is the same that is now pressed upon the acceptance of congregations in Christian lands. It may, by reason of human defects, be at times disfigured;—the ignorance of the preacher and the unpreparedness of the people, often doubtless prevent such wonderful effects as were witnessed in Pentecostal times, but surely some churches hold the truth, and present the truth with sufficient distinctness and correctness to profit any candid hearer. It cannot be, that throughout Christendom there is to be found no church organization suited to your taste, and no pulpit where the Gospel in all its native simplicity and power is preached! Surely no man is vain enough to imagine that in intellectual power and spiritual experience, and biblical knowledge, he is in advance of anything the church contains within her ranks;—that he combines in his own person all the orthodoxy, all the learning, and all the wisdom of the past, and can gain no new ideas, and no heavenly unction, by fellowship with the Church of Christ! And yet such, in effect, is what many singularly constructed Christians say at the present day. No church quite meets their approval. They cannot endure the formalism and ceremonial display of Episcopal Churches. They cannot stand the extravagance and unregulated enthusiasm of the Methodists. They condemn the narrowness—the bigotry—the exclusiveness of the Baptists. They complain of the coldness and stiffness of Presbyterians, and they cannot sympathize with the laxity of discipline which prevails in Congregational Churches! Surely such conduct, and such sentiments, prove the existence of a large amount of spiritual pride, coupled with an exceeding childishness of temperament unbecoming intelligent men. It is the old complaint of the Jews in the time of Christ: "We have piped unto you and ye have not danced; we have mourned unto you, and ye have not lamented."

I have, so far, charitably supposed that the class of persons discribed are really anxious about religion, but, from some most unfortunate warp in their constitution, are thus disaffected towards all Churches and all ecclesiastical organisations. I fear however that we regard them too tenderly, and that other less honorable motives may account for such singular conduct. There are many to be found who respect religion and ministers of the Gospel only so far as they can turn them to some account in the furtherance of their own selfish plans and projects. They have marked out for themselves a certain course in life, and anything that interferes with its successful accomplishment must be attacked and calumniated, be the means the most unscrupulous and unjust. The Jews in the time of Christ had little relish for religious topics. Some of them did profess to seek after a higher life, but the great mass were bent upon the material pleasures and enjoyments of the age, and any form of religion that rebuked such carnality was looked upon as out of place. If they could not use John the Baptist and Jesus Christ to the furtherance of their own sinful and selfish designs;—if they would not join with them in their false and frivolous pursuits, or at least wink at their follies, then they must endeavour to injure their reputation and malign their doctrine. Had Christ really been the glutton and drunkard they declared He was—had He consorted with them in their revelries and pleasures, and lowered His morality to suit their wishes, He would have had thousands of followers and friends from the ranks of these same

Jews. It was because His life and His teaching was a standing rebuke of all their evil practices that He was made the object of such groundless aspersions.

Is this the secret of modern opposition to ministers and churches? Is it this that the Saviour foretold when He said "If they call the master of the house Beelzebub, how much more shall they call them of his household?" Have we indeed any right to expect but that, just in proportion as we are faithful to the trust committed to us, our language and our lives shall be misconstrued—misunderstood—and misapplied? If the ministers of religion will not modify their teaching to meet the fluctuating opinions of the world, what can they expect but insult and misrepresentation? If the doctrine is disliked, the teacher must be abused. If men's secret sins and public dishonesties are fearlessly attacked, what more easy or more natural than to cry out against all existing religious organizations and all orders of the ministry. The real cause is never avowed—that would hardly be prudent, nor is it necessary when so many excuses and charges can be made. At times it is the expense of churches—the continual demands that are made for benevolent enterprises. At other times the self-righteous attitude of church members — their exclusivsness and illiberality towards the outside world. At other times it is the preacher himself. His sermons are too long or too short; he is too doctrinal or too practical;—he is too abstract or too sentimental;—the flimsiest reason is laid hold of to reject the Gospel and neglect its requirements. If he insists strongly on purity of life and sanctity of thought, then it is said he is too strict—righteous over much, always demanding a style of life and conduct beyond the reach of fallible mortals in a fallen world. If he is cheerful, happy and mirthful in his disposition, and familar in his address, he is stigmatized as light and frivolous—as wanting in that gravity and dignity becoming a servant of Christ. If he is grave, and strict, and sombre in his deportment, then he is described as gloomy and sour— puritanical and narrow - minded. If he eats and drinks and dresses like other people—if he enters with spirit into the innocent enjoyments of life, then the world says he is nothing different or better than themselves, and that his religion is but a form. Preach as he may—live as he may—no minister of Christ can be above the reproach of worldly men; for, as an old commentator says, "Whatever measures good men take, they will never escape the censures of the world. The best way is not to be concerned at them." To such men even the sweetness of the honey comb would seem distasteful.

Now, are there in this congregation, either as stated or occasional hearers, any of the classes I have described? Do not, I beseech you, be too ready to censure the Church or the preacher. Look within and see if there be not something essentially wrong, either with the head or with the heart. You may be like the sick patient, of whom I spoke in the opening of my remarks, under the influence of a disease, that perverts your taste and destroys your power of perception. The carnal mind knoweth not the things of the Spirit—they are spiritually discerned: Divine illumination is needed before they can be appreciated or relished. You are the victim of moral obliquity. You are neither honest in your judgments, nor sincere in your search after truth.

Unless conscience has already been overpowered and perverted beyond recovery, it must at times convic you of unjust and censorious criticisms; of numerous occasions when you have laid hold of the imperfections of churches and ministers and office-bearers, to cover over or palliate gross direlictions of duty and manifest wrong-doing in life. I caution you against continuing in such a course of conduct. Were the errors of the Church and the evils of the ministry a thousand-fold more numerous and aggravated than they are, they would not in the least extenuate your guilt. At the bar of God no man can roll over his sins on the shoulders of another, or blame the deficiencies of human agencies for his wilful neglect of ordinances. I know of no evangelical church at the present day that does not afford blessed opportunity for spiritual improvement, and ample room for the exercise ot the noblest talents, and the most exalted graces. Woe be to the man who refuses to enter upon the cultivation of his spiritual energies because of petty and insignificant details, either in the discipline or in the doctrine of the Church. Better for him he had never heard a sermon, and never enjoyed the advantages of Christian civilization. "Woe unto thee, Chorazim! Woe unto thee, Bethsaida! for if the mighty works which were done in you had been done in Tyre and Sidon, they would have repented long ago in sackcloth and ashes."

Once for all, let it be understood we cannot lower the · demands and obligations of our holy religion. Whether men will hear, or forbear, we must maintain, in all its integrity and purity, the fundamental principles of our faith. Fidelity to our Master—love for souls—and a sense of our accountability at the bar of God, forbid all tampering with unhallowed pleasures, and all conformity to worldly maxims. Let our names be despised, our characters traduced, our reputations depreciated, all, and much more, rather than we should incur the displeasure of Almighty God. Better far the testimony of a good conscience and the favour of the Master, than the applause and commendation of the worldly and profane.

Finally let me say to every hearer of the Gospel:

"Look to thy actions well,
For churches either are our heaven or hell

The Blessedness of the Godly Man.

"He shall dwell on high; his place of defence shall be the munitions of rocks; bread shall be given him, his waters shall be sure."—ISAIAH xxxiii. 16.

From the 29th to the 33rd chapters of this prophecy, an account is given of the distress that was to follow the invasion of Sennacherib. In the midst of these national trials and calamities, Divine interposition is promised. God is to arise against the enemies of His Church and people, and work out for them a mighty deliverance. At the very moment when all hope is despaired of—when the highways lie waste, and the wayfaring man ceases; when the earth languishes and mourns—when Lebanon is ashamed and hewn down—when Sharon is like a wilderness, and Bashan and Carmel shake off their fruits, then, saith the Lord, "will I arise and be exalted; then will I lift up Myself." The effect of these singular deliverances from the hand of God upon the enemies of the Jews, and upon impenitent sinners in Jerusalem, in view of God's judgments upon the army of Sennacherib, is described in the context: "The sinners in Zion are afraid; fearfulness hath surprised the hypocrites; Who among us shall dwell with the devouring fire? Who among us shall dwell with everlasting burnings?" Finally there is presented us a glowing picture of the character and blessedness of the truly pious man. "He that walketh righteously and speaketh uprightly; he that despiseth the gain of oppressions, that shaketh his hands from holding of bribes, that closeth his ears from hearing of blood, and shutteth his eyes from seeing evil—*this man shall dwell on high*;—in the midst of all these commotions and agitations he shall remain unmoved; the thunders and lightnings of God's vengeance shall harm him not; amid the overthrow of empires, and the downfall of kingdoms, he shall maintain a cheerful confidence in the protection of Heaven." "He shall dwell on High; his place of defence shall be the munitions of rocks; bread shall be given him; his water shall be sure."

We propose to enlarge the text and give it a world-wide application. In considering it, we shall perhaps discover why it is that God's people maintain the utmost tranquility and serenity of mind in the midst of alarming tokens of God's presence; why it is that when worldly and irreligious men and sceptics are blaspheming, and statesmen and politicians are despairing of the safety of the commonwealth, and all ranks and classes of men are rocked hither and thither by evil tidings, that the godly man alone, continues calm and collected as in more peaceful times. "He dwells on high; his place of defence is the munition of rocks."

These three points claim our attention.

1. The godly man's dwelling. He shall dwell on high, in heights or high places.

2. The godly man's defence. His place of defence shall be the munition of rocks.

3. The godly man's provision. Bread shall be given him; his water shall be sure.

1. *The godly man's dwelling.* "He shall dwell on high," beyond the reach of storms and tempests; and far removed from this lower world. Faint

echoes of its tumults and social earthquakes may at times reach his ears, like the low dull muttering of the distant thunder-peal, as it dies away amid the mountain solitudes; but they disturb not his serenity. The peace of God that passeth all understanding, keeps his heart and mind. He can say, "God is my refuge and strength a very present help in trouble; therefore will I not fear, though the earth be removed, and though the mountains be carried into the midst of the sea. Though the waters thereof roar and be troubled, and though the mountains shake with the swelling thereof."

It is worthy of note, how frequently in the Old Testament Scriptures God is spoken of, as the refuge of His saints in troublous times. In periods when persecution and trials for the sake of righteousness abounded, and national judgments prevailed, the prophets and saints of God lived in an atmosphere free from anxiety and sorrow in their over mastering forms. Their strong faith lifted them up to a place of calm, whence, amid confusion and agitation, they recognized and reposed in the sover-

eignty of God. In such dark hours their souls
gathered strength and fortitude by the memory of
former days, when Jehovah triumphed gloriously
over all His enemies, and scattered by His breath
the foes of His Church and people.

It is the privilege of God's children now as
then, "to dwell on high." "Oh! that I had wings
like a dove, for then would I fly away and be at
rest," is frequently the cry of the soul oppressed
with varied sorrows. Are there not times when
the calamities of life seem too heavy to be borne,
and we sink outright in the deep waters of affliction, saying, like the Psalmist of old, "All thy
waves and thy billows are gone over me?" Seeing
no relief on either hand, and allowing our fears to
overcome our faith, we would gladly give up the
conflict and pass beyond the reach of sin and sorrow, "where the wicked cease from troubling and
the weary are at rest." But such helpless despondency and despair is not the part of true wisdom.
It is possible, amid the conflict and struggle of
existence, to enjoy hallowed and refreshing communion with God. Amid the commotions and

revolutions which shake society to its very foundations, and cause the stoutest hearts to quake and tremble, we may repose with confidence in the mysterious workings of the Almighty, all whose dealings are marked by matchless love. Then it is that we are "to dwell on high," saying with the Psalmist; "Though an host should encamp against me, my heart shall not fear; though war should rise against me, in this will I be confident. * * * In the time of trouble He shall hide me in His pavilion; in the secret of His tabernacle shall He hide me; He shall set me up upon a rock." He that dwelleth in the secret place of the Most High shall abide under the shadow of the Almighty. Thou shalt not be afraid for the terror by night, nor the arrow that flieth by day. Thou shalt hide them in secret of Thy presence from the pride of man; Thou shalt keep them secretly in a pavilion from the strife of tongues." There are no cares in the higher experience of the Christian life, as there is no dust in the upper atmosphere. We are told that near the city of Naples, there is a grotto that exhales carbonic acid gas. Being heavier than the air, the gas lies in a thin stratum clos to the ground, so that animals walking near the surface are at once killed, while an upright man experiences no injury. So it is with the sorrows and cares of life. If we lie down under them, we are poisoned and suffocated. If we stand erect in the sunshine of Heaven, and in the light of God's countenance, we inhale the pure air, and become all the stronger by the discipline of trial.

But more is implied than a mere temporary refuge. The words denote a permanent place of shelter. "He shall *dwell* on high;" not merely lodge, as a wayfaring man, for a night, but make it his abode. It is a place where the soul has its home—where at all times it is certain of a refuge. "Lord thou hast been *our dwelling place* in all generations," is the language of the godly man. There are some men who deem it sufficient to have a covert when danger threatens, and who are only driven to solemn thoughts by God's providences, and when human resources fail. They are like homeless, friendless vagrants, or helpless orphans, who wander from door to door, destitute of family joys and parental love. They know nothing of the hallowed endearments and the sacred delights of the domestic circle, whose members are bound together by the golden ties of a sincere affection. But it is otherwise with the Christian. God is his dwelling place and refuge in the changing scenes of life. "I am continually with thee," is his language; "Thou shalt guide me with Thy counsel, and afterward receive me into glory." Thus the good man's communion is on high — his interest lies beyond the present—the body is on the earth, but the soul is in Heaven. His emotions—his affections and all the nobler aspirations of his nature tend upwards, and from thence proceeds all his comforts, hopes, and consolations.

Finally, may we not understand the words to mean, that, from this high elevation, the soul can look down upon this arena of mortal conflict and comprehend the glorious issue of the contest. Just as on some lofty mountain-top, far above the walls and battlements of the city, and removed from the smoke and dust, and vapours that obstruct the view in its crowded thoroughfares, the traveller can take in the beauty of the landscape, and penetrate for miles the vastness and loveliness of the ever widening horizon, so is it with the Christian's faith, in regard to mysterious providences and strange events. Are there not moments in his history, when, as in Jacob's vision, ladders are seen reaching heavenward, and unfolding before his rapt vision God's dealing in the future with the Church and world? Are there not periods when God takes away his people from the toilsome journey of the wilderness, up to Pisgah heights, whence they can survey the promised land, and anticipate a glorious victory? Are there not seasons when, like Paul and the beloved apostle John, the Holy Spirit spreads out before them in panoramic view, the hopes and happiness of the future world? In such moments they "dwell on high."

Everything depends upon our point of observation, in beholding natural distances. If you want a grand view of the city and surrounding landscape, you must climb some lofty spire. And when military commanders would understand the position and resources of the enemy, they ascend in balloons far above the dense foliage of the forest. So when we would understand anything concerning God's dealings with this world—the reasons why He permits so much sin and wretchedness, and why men's passions boil and foam like so many heated cauldrons, and why, for so many centuries, evil has been allowed to claim the mastery over good—we must take a higher elevation, and seek a better point of vision, than this lower world. Thus only can we form an estimate of God's dealings with our-race, and possess our souls in patience. "The secret of the Lord is with them that fear Him, and He will show them His covenant."

The higher we ascend above the surface of the earth, the more insignificant do its details appear. Looked upon from the verge of some far-off world, this vast globe of ours is but a paltry insignificant speck in space. And in like manner, the higher the Christian rises above the tumults and agitations of life, the less does he value its pleasures and amusements. What seem to other men of great importance, are petty and unsatisfying in his eyes. He measures them in the light of eternity, and as they effect his immortality! "He dwells on high."

2. *The godly man's defence.* " His place of defence shall be the munitions of rocks." This denotes complete security. It is not a fortification of earthworks, hastily thrown up, and as easily thrown down;—nor is it one of masonry, however skilfully constructed by human art;—but it is a munition of rocks, strong and high, and bidding defiance alike to the cannon-ball, the desolating tempest and ocean's fury. The eagle builds her nest among rocky crags and slanting precipices, but even there she is not free from danger. Human daring, in the face of fearful obstacles, invades her nest, and robs her of her treasures. But those whom God protects need fear neither the assaults of man, nor the attack of devils. "The gates of hell cannot prevail against them."

This is a comforting truth, and one often presented in Scripture. "They that trust in the Lord shall be as Mount Zion, which cannot be removed, but abideth forever. As the mountains are round about Jerusalem, so the Lord is round about His people from henceforth and forever. In that day shall this song be sung in the land of. Judah!

We have a strong city; salvation will God appoint for walls and bulwarks. * * * Trust ye in the Lord forever; for in the Lord Jehovah is everlasting strength. * * * And a man shall be as a hiding-place from the wind, as a covert from the tempest; as rivers of water in a dry place; as the shadow of a great rock in a weary land." And Moses, in taking farewell of the children of Israel, says, "The eternal God is thy refuge, and underneath thee are the everlasting arms. Who is like unto thee, O people, saved by the Lord?" Nor is it simply that God defends His people collectively, but that He exercises a special protection over individual believers. When God permitted Satan to tempt His servant Job, Satan used the significant language: "Hast thou not made an hedge about him and about his house, and about all that he hath on every side," implying that in his case, and in the case of the humblest believer, there is the constant regard of an ever-watchful Providence. "The angel of the Lord encampeth round about them that fear Him, and delivereth them." There is a place in His loving heart for every member of His Church.

There is, I fear, much practical unbelief among Christians on this subject. They are willing to believe that the Church is founded upon a rock— that God defends and fortifies the cause of truth and righteousness against every foe—but they are slow to believe that He stands sentinel for every believer, and that there is an actual outstretching of His arm, in defending him against sudden temptations and dangers, just as there is a constant supervision and exercise of Almighty power in sustaining those suns and systems that revolve in space. But such is the doctrine of Scripture. God not only rocks the cradle of the universe, but rocks the cradle of every believer it contains. There is no trial or temptation that can prevail without His knowledge, or against His will.

It is not as an abstract theoretical dogma that I present this fact. It is not that you may simply believe and admire the wonderful comprehensiveness of that Providence which singles out souls from the infinity of existence, and makes them th object of His solicitude, but that you may realize the comfort that flows from such a truth in every situation of life. If I am assured of Divine protection in every time of danger, of safety from every peril, and victory over every enemy, what need is there for alarm in the darkest and most trying situations of life? With God for their defence

> "The saints securely sing
> Defiance to the gates of hell."

3. *The godly man's provision.* "Bread shall be given him, his waters shall be sure." It is not a matter of doubt or mere probability. The language is that of absolute certainty. "Bread *shall* be given." "The young lions may lack and suffer hunger, but they that seek the Lord *shall not* want any good thing. I have been young, and now am old: yet have I never seen the righteous forsaken, nor his seed begging bread."

Oftentimes the Christian's daily provision seems exceedingly precarious, but it is only so to human eyes. God provides just as emergencies arise, and in these instances by very mysterious and unexpected channels. Hagar in the wilderness, when the bottle was spent, cast her child from her under the shrubs, and laid herself down to die, when lo! near at hand there was a sparkling fountain to quench her thirst and sustain the life of her child. The Israelites in their journeyings had no flour for bread, but daily supplies of Heaven-prepared manna, and abundant flocks of quail, and living streams of water from the flinty rock, supplied their every want. Elijah hides himself by the brook Cherith, and drinks of the water of the stream, and morning and evening eats flesh and bread brought him by the ravens. Again, when, wearied of life, he lies down under the juniper tree, eagerly desiring that God would end his days, an angel touches him and tells him to rise and eat. And are there not in the experience of many Christians at the present day, not less wonderful examples of how God provides for the temporal necessities of His people? Why, then, should God's saints burden themselves by fears of want? Take no thought for your life —no unnecessary or sinful forebodings—as to what ye shall eat, or what ye shall drink, nor yet as to your body, what ye shall put on. "Behold the fowls of the air, for they sow not, neither do they reap nor gather into barns; yet your heavenly Father feedeth them! Are ye not much better than they? Therefore if God so clothe the grass of the field, which to-day is, and to-morrow is cast into the oven, shall He not much more clothe you, O ye of little faith?"

It is altogether a wrong idea that God cares but little for the temporal or physical welfare of His children, and that His only concern is their higher and immortal nature. The text, and other passages of Scripture, clearly teach that His sympathies are enlisted in all that belongs to the present well-being of His saints, and that He understands and cares for our bodily ailments and infirmities with greater constancy than that of the fondest mother who weeps in sorrow over the sufferings and untold necessities of her helpless babe. There are periods when we are made to feel our absolute dependence upon Providence for daily bread. For the most part our common mercies come to us so regularly, and want is so seldom in our homes, that we fail to value the constant gifts of Heaven. It is only when, by some national calamity, the wheels of commerce are suddenly stopped, or the productions of the field cease to grow, and the mildew of Heaven wastes our borders, and famine and pestilence with all their attendant horrors press upon the land, that we feel the literal truth, that in God we live, and move, and have our being. Then we are led to serious reflection upon God's unfailing mercies and man's ingratitude, and then it is that we can plead, if we are God's children, the promise of the text, that bread shall be given us, and that our waters shall be sure.

But mark that nothing is promised but the bare necessaries of life. God can give us more—may give us more—very frequently He does give us more, but in every such case He goes beyond the terms of His promise. Even these necessaries of life far exceed the merits of the most deserving, and should His wisdom see fit to give us nothing more, we must rest submissive. This world is but a prison, and as long as we are in it we must rest contented with prison fare.

But bread and water evidently include all spiritual blessings needed in our earthly pilgrimage.

These terms are often used as symbols of the higher wants of the soul, and surely, if God provides for our poor decaying bodies, He will most certainly provide for our higher natures. Every gift and grace will be most freely bestowed;—"the Lord will give grace and glory, and no good thing will He withhold from them that walk uprightly." The body is but the casket of the soul, which demands higher nourishment than the bread that perisheth, and just as the body languishes and dies without material subsistence, so, without the constant nourishment of God's spirit, our higher life becomes feeble and torpid. In the history and progress of the soul there are ever increasing and enlarging desires. If there is spiritual health, there will be no complete satisfying of the soul's demands on this side of eternity. To-day's supplies will but whet the appetite for to-morrow's blessings. And thus it is that faith and dependence upon God are developed in Christian character. He gives us no superfluous graces, but He meets our demands from time to time as they arise, saying, "My grace is sufficient for thee—My strength shall be perfected in thy weakness. Thy shoes shall be iron and

brass; and as thy days so shall thy strength be."
Or, as Paul writes to the Philippians: "My God
shall supply all your need, according to His riches
in glory by Christ Jesus."

I am prepared to hear some child of God candidly reply, that the promise of the text, "Bread shall be given him, his waters shall be sure," has often failed. In their own experience it has not always held good. They have passed through days of privation and penury, when the crust of bread and cup of water, and cruse of oil, have been hard to find, and when their hearts sunk within them as their children cried because of the pangs of hunger. The Christian minister and physician meet such cases too frequently, even in our so-called land of plenty, where, from fraud, indolence, or evil-doing on the part of a parent, or from the death of a pious husband, poverty and starvation become a sad experience. God's children are by no means exempted from such trials. Often they appear marked out for them beyond the average of humanity. Industry and toil—honesty and integrity—do not always meet with their natural and just reward.

"Man's inhumanity to man," continues, as of old, to make "countless thousands mourn." And yet, though to human observation the promise of my text may not in every case have been so palpably and quickly carried out, as human nature would desire, how frequently has the needed provision come in such a mysterious way, and at such a time, as proved beyond all doubt, that the covenant stands sure, and the Lord can never forsake His saints. By human agents, mysteriously sent in our hours of need, and as really the messengers of Heaven as were the angels to needy saints, "our bread has been given us, and our waters have been sure." Thus, like Israel of old, divinely sustained and provided for in the pathless desert, each Christian can sing:

> "Lord, 'tis enough, I ask no more;
> These blessings are Divine—
> I envy not the worldling's store,
> Since Christ and Heaven are mine."

Some here know nothing of this blessedness! They have no such dwelling—no such defence—no such promise. Recipients of God's common bounties, they have no part in the bestowments of covenant love. Into those higher experiences of Christian life they have never entered. Material delights and transitory pleasures fill up the plan of existence. O pitiable condition! a soul destined to live forever, without God's favour here or presence hereafter. It need not be so. Come, ye famishing souls —partake of the free and ever-flowing fountain of God's love, and let your souls delight in fatness. "He that eateth of this bread shall live forever."

"As a Weaned Child."

"My soul is even as a weaned child."—PSALM cxxxi. 2.

The translation of the text fails to give us the force of the original. It is as if the Psalmist David said, "God knows, if I have not soothed and quieted my soul, as a child weaned from its mother." It is the language of strong asseveration; an appeal to God for the sincerity of his feelings and the truth of his declarations. In other portions of God's word, the state of mind represented by the term "weaned," is spoken of by such a phrase as "spiritual-mindedness;"—that stage in the Christian's experience when the believer becomes entirely indifferent to the outward and tangible realities of life, so far as finding in them a source of lasting comfort or enjoyment. We may endeavour faintly to describe what is meant by the text, but the believer only can fully comprehend the thing itself.

"A weaned child" is one that has ceased to use the mother's milk. For a certain period of the child's existence, unless in exceptional cases, the child depends upon the mother's milk for strength and sustenance, and can be satisfied with nothing else. Deny it this nourishment and it dies; continue it until a certain period of its life, and the child grows up strong and healthy. The time comes, however, when the child must be weaned from its mother's breast, and other and more solid food substituted for the mother's milk. But to bring the child to forget what it formerly loved, and imperatively demanded from hour to hour, is often a protracted labour. The child cannot understand this sudden change in the mother's conduct—doubtless it thinks such treatment harsh and cruel—and unless there is firmness and resolution on the parent's part to persevere until the process is accomplished, the child, by its earnest solicitations and touching plaints, may for a period protract the struggle. At last, however, the child is compelled by hunger to take some other food, which it soon begins to relish and seek for, as it formerly did for the mother's milk. Now, says the Psalmist, just as the child becomes utterly indifferent and regardless of the means of subsistence provided for its earliest and most helpless stage of existence, so do I feel with regard to the more common carnal delights and luxuries of life. Humility has taken the place of former pride and haughtiness. Instead of the low, grovelling ambitions that for the most part engage the attention of men, aspirations, heavenly in their nature, and divinely inspired, fill and fire my soul. My will, which was formerly under no restraint whatever—perverse, defiant, and ungovernable—is now completely subjected to the will and authority of a higher and a nobler power; in a word, my whole character is so radically changed that I can imagine nothing in nature which so suitably and strikingly represents my altered condiion as that of a "weaned child." Or in the words of the Christian Poet, describing the complete surrender of the whole being to the service of Christ;

> "People of the living God,
> I have sought the world around,
> Paths of sin and sorrow trod,
> Peace and comfort nowhere found.
> Now to you my spirit turns,
> Turns, a fugitive unblest;
> Brethren, where your altar burns
> O receive me into rest.

"Lonely I no longer roam,
Like the cloud, the wind, the wave,
Where you dwell shall be my home,
Where you die shall be my grave;
Mine the God whom you adore,
Your Redeemer shall be mine,
Earth can fill my soul no more,
Every idol I resign."

Now I need not say that such feelings, and such an unreserved surrender of earthly enjoyments and earthly idols, is by no means natural to man. The world, and the things that are in the world; the lust of the flesh, the lust of the eyes, and the pride of life, form the chief objects of attraction. Withdraw the mass of men from such pursuits and pleasures, and you render life unbearable, and existence a very burden. I do not say that all unconverted and unregenerate men are equally the creatures of sense, but the world in some form or other is their all in all. In one case it is the enjoyment of sensual pleasure, in another the pursuit of wealth, in another the desire of fame, in another the love of power, that claims the sympathies and active energies of mankind. So completely wrapped up in the friendships and delights of the present world are many men, that they can hardly afford the holy rest of one day in seven for the service of their Maker and preparation for Heaven. The Sabbath is to them a weariness; the hours outwardly spent in exercises of devotion are in reality devoted to the conception of new plans and enterprises whereby they may buy and sell and get gain. God is not in all their thoughts, and the solemn concerns of eternity have no bearing whatever upon their lives. Such men are hardly ever "weaned" from the world, until Death violently snaps asunder the bond which unites soul and body, and ushers the spirit into the realities of the unseen world.

This, you may say, is the extreme of worldliness. Be it so; it is one of the tendencies of the age, and a too common characteristic of professing Christians. The other extreme, against which I warn you as entirely unscriptural and unnatural in a healthy Christian, is a certain extreme spirituality of mind, which affects to look down with horror and disdain upon the more innocent pleasures and enjoyments of life, and, in some cases, causes good men to withdraw from active intercourse with their fellow men. There are some Christians who are continually mourning over the degeneracy of the age—the fearful dishonesties practised in business—the spirit of worldliness that is creeping into the Church of Christ—and the absence of vital piety in the lives of God's people;—all which is perhaps too true and to be regretted. But the most hopeful plan of correcting such flagrant evils in the world is certainly not by withdrawing from the obligations of life and the performance of those duties which an all-wise Providence imposes upon every creature of His hand. We are not angels; and while in the world our employments cannot be entirely angelic. We do not as yet possess spiritual bodies, and therefore, to sustain these bodies, we must for a while depend upon the grosser elements of existence. We are not yet enrolled among the happy number of the redeemed in Heaven, and therefore our time cannot be entirely devoted to the exercise of prayer and praise. So long as we are in the wilderness we must toil, struggle, buy and sell, make provision against future wants, and by all laudable means maintain our respectability and honour before the world. I have no sympathy whatever with those men who are so exceedingly holy in their own eyes that they fear contamination with their fellow mortals. There is something fearfully out of joint in that man's religious experience who sees nothing to commend in the ordinary business of life, and learns no lessons of practical and lasting value by intercourse with his fellow men. What the Bible demands of us is, not cessation from active duty, but the mingling of religion in every act, and the consecration of every calling to the glory of God. Nor do I sympathize with a certain class of professing Christians who frown upon all those innocent and healthful pleasures that help to oil the machinery of life, and make men more vigorous and happy in the discharge of duty, and in the endurance of trials. Every part of our nature, I take it, should be cultivated, and only in so far as we thus fulfil the Divine purpose can we preserve a due equipoise between soul and body. The devil must not monopolize all the mirth, and geniality, and pure enjoyments of the world. These must be made subordinate to the higher purposes of existence, but at the same time useful auxiliaries to a religious life. When a man or woman joins the

Church of Christ, it does not follow that they are to assume a morose and rueful countenance, and practice the asceticism of the dark ages, when the walls of monasteries and nunneries, raised high as Heaven, endeavoured by material force to make men spiritually-minded. All secular good things belong to the Christian. He is to use this world in the highest and noblest sense. He has a perfect right to surround himself with the treasures of art and refinement, and make this beautiful world minister to the finer affections of his nature;—to enjoy the melody of music, and listen to the highest efforts of cultivated genius. The Christian's home should be a constant scene of holy joy—bright, cheerful, and radiant with sunny smiles; and the Christian's countenance and conversation among his fellow men a source of happiness and an ever-flowing fountain of refreshment. As has been truly said, "Conscience is good—veneration is good—and solemnity is good; but cheerfulness is just as good and as necessary in the human soul. It is the blessed spirit that God has set in the mind to dust it, and to enliven its dark places. Praying can no more be made a substitute for smiling, than smiling can for praying."

You see then, my hearers, that in exhorting you to "weanedness" from the world, and a closer walk with God, I demand nothing incompatible with the full development of all these powers and affections which have been wisely implanted in the soul. I only ask that the things of the present world be held in abeyance to the things of eternity—that we do not forget that, after all, our stay on earth is brief, and that all our enjoyments here must have a bearing upon our state hereafter. "Brethren, the time is short —it remaineth that they that have wives, be as though they had none; and they that weep as though they wept not; and they that rejoice as though they rejoiced not; and they that buy as though they possessed not, and they that use this world, as not abusing it; for the fashion of this world passeth away."

Let me briefly describe, then, the character of a man who is weaned from the world:—*First*—While none the less sensible of the many sources of enjoyment that this present world affords, he has become more alive to the value of spiritual and eternal realities. He does not less love and enjoy the things of time, but more intensely grasps the felicities of the future. He has found Christ, and with Christ such rich and precious promises of blessedness beyond the grave, that he is more indifferent to the changes and vicissitudes of earth. The reality hides the shadow—the possession the promise. He is not disgusted with the world, although he is weaned from it, but, in comparison with its highest enjoyments, the present inner delights, and prospective glories of Heaven, seem far better fitted to his immortal nature. He can say, "Whom have I in Heaven but Thee? and there is none on earth that I desire beside Thee." "As for me, I will behold Thy face in righteousness; I shall be satisfied when I awake with Thy likeness." "There may be many that say, Who will show us any good? Lord lift Thou up the light of Thy countenance upon us." "Thou hast put gladness into my heart, more than in the time that their corn and their wine is increased." Faith thus becomes to the Christian actual possession. "It is not only a spiritual insight, but a realizing appropriating faculty, through which God, and, with Him, all things become his." Or, as Hartley Coleridge beautifully and philosophically puts it,

"Think not the faith, by which the just shall live,
Is a dead creed, a map correct of Heaven,
Far less a feeling fond and fugitive,
A thoughtless gift, withdrawn as soon as given.
It is an affirmation and an act
That bids eternal truth be present fact."

Second—Thus alive to the value of spiritual and eternal realities, the enjoyments and material comforts of the present are the less necessary to his well-being. I do not say *entirely unnecessary*, for I take it that no man gets so etherealized in this world as to be entirely independent of many of the more common conditions of existence. But a state of mind is produced that is far less affected by the changes of fortune, and the trials incident to mortality, than is usual in the carnal heart. The enjoyment of a greater good—or, if you will, the promise of such greater good in the future—subdues all desires and relish after loss. No man who has drunk deeply of the inexhaustible treasures of God's grace can be satisfied with the intermittent streams of earthly pleasures, or waste his time in hewing out broken cisterns that can hold no water. The deep-seated yearnings of the human soul, and those strong spiritual instincts that from time to time wake suddenly in the breast, "like infants from their sleep—who stretch their arms into the dark and weep," can only be satisfied in God; and, once satisfied, what can trials and disappointments do to disturb our tranquility and serenity of mind? "He's posses't of Heaven, who Heaven hath within his breast." In childhood, how highly prized are the toys and playthings that affection provides for the amusement and development of the opening mind. In boyhood and girlhood more advanced amusements and enjoyments are provided to meet the growing tasks and kindling intelligence, until, casting aside the more childish as well as the more matured pastimes of early life, we reach the period of manhood, and consign to fairy dreamland all the fictions of our earlier years. The little hillock that then seemed a very mountain, now assumes its just proportions; the little village church, that appeared a grand and gorgeous edifice, now appears a very rude and homely pile of stones; the men and women whose daily conversation seemed so wonderful, and whose proverbs seemed so wise, now become very ordinary mortals in our estimation. And yet no change has taken place in these different objects of youthful interest;—the change is in ourselves. Age—experience—a more extended acquaintance with society;—ability to measure things at a truer value, have depreciated them in our eyes. The enthusiasm of youth has given place to the solid judgment of manhood. So it is with the man who is "weaned" from the world. He has tasted the powers of the world to come, and now longs to enjoy more perfectly what Faith tells him is in reserve. His heart has been changed, and his tastes have been changed. Born of the Spirit, he now seeks after the things of the Spirit, and can say like the Apostle Paul, "Yea, doubtless, and I count all things but loss, for the excellency of the knowledge of Christ Jesus my Lord."

> "I thirst, but not as once I did,
> The vain delights of earth to share,
> Thy wounds, Emmanuel, all forbid
> That I should seek my pleasure there.
>
> "It was the sight of Thy dear cross
> First weaned my soul from earthly things,
> And taught me to esteem as dross
> The mirth of fools and pomp of kings."

I should now briefly speak of the means by which the spiritual change is effected. "Weaning" the soul from this world is always God's work. By no efforts of our own, *unaided*, can we accomplish it. Neither by vigils, or penances, or fasts, or lacerations of the body, or pilgrimages to the shrines of saints, can we produce this Heavenly - mindedness. Afflictions cannot in themselves wean us from this world. Many a man who has lain upon a bed of sickness, and has been brought to the very verge of the spirit - world, has come back to life more intensely avaricious and grasping than ever. The promises of leading a new life, made in the hour of anguish, have all evaporated on the return of health, and under the sunshine of prosperity. Nor will mere experience of the hollowness and vanity of all created hopes convert the heart and wean it from the world. How, then, can a man be brought to say, "My soul is even as a weaned child?"

First—I answer, God weans believers from this world by sore afflictions and successive bereavements, thus teaching them the transitory and unsatisfactory nature of worldly enjoyments. It needs not one, but *oft - repeated strokes* to transfer the affections of the human soul from the carnal enjoyments and pleasures of life, and centre them upon God Himself. "The natural man dies hard within us," and the man from heaven is not born without a pang. And even after the soul has forsaken all the grosser and more repulsive excitements of this world, much yet remains in producing that implicit reliance upon the Saviour, and that strong confidence in the hopes and promises of Scripture, which form the source of all true spiritual mindedness. The members of our family circles—the partners of our blood—the children of our households, in many cases monopolize the love and affection that belongs to God, and divide our allegiance and consecration. Instead of making them but stepping-stones or links by which we may become more closely united to our Maker, and give to Him an homage and love altogether different from what we bestow on the creature, we stop short in the range, and sweep off these affections, and bestow upon mere flesh and blood, what was originally intended for Heaven and Heavenly felicities. And in many cases it is only by repeated trials and losses that the soul is brought nearer and nearer to its God, while at the same time it begins to see how unsubstantial are all the poor unrealities of time. It is the pressure of calamity that developes true strength and heroism of character, just as the stress and strain of the tempest seems but to sink the roots of the giant oak more firmly in the earth. Little coffins, in which there lie the hopes and idols of fathers and mothers, become often, under God's blessing, the most eloquent of preachers, and the most sanctifying of all agencies. "By these keen desolating shocks, like the blasting of the breath of God's chiding, are the deep foundations of our nature discovered to us. When the veil of the temple, even the poor worn garment of our humanity, is rent from the top to the bottom, we catch glimpses of the inner glory—the rocks are riven—the graves open, they who have long slept in the dust come forth, and reveal to us awful and tender secrets of which otherwise we should have known nothing." St. Chrysostom beautifully remarks that "there are joys which spring out of the very heart of anguish—and pale flowers which thrust themselves out of the ruins of hope—of endeavour and affection—breathing a deeper and sweeter fragrance than the broad wealth of air and sunshine ever gave." Many in this congregation, by sad experience, know how true are the words of the Christian poet when he says,

> "The stricken heart bereft
> Of all its brood of singing hopes, and left
> 'Mid leafless boughs, a cold, forsaken nest
> With snow flakes in it, folded in thy breast
> Doth lose its deadly chill; and grief that creeps
> Unto thy side for shelter, finding there
> The wounds deep cleft, forgets its moan, and weeps
> Calm, quiet tears; and on thy forehead care
> Hath looked, until its thorns, no longer bare,
> Put forth pale roses."

Second—By *crosses and disappointments, and failures in business*, God weans His people from the world. Poverty of means, and poverty of souls do not always go together. Often it is the reverse. The heart is often the most prosperous spiritually, when the outward life and circumstances of the believer are most adverse. The Bible, it is true, lays down the general principle, that godliness is profitable for all' things, both for the present world and that which is to come, and that, if we seek first the kingdom of God, and His righteousness, all other things shall be added thereto. But this in no way conflicts with the fact that many of the best of men never reach a position of affluence, or even comfort in this world. Their whole existence is one long continued struggle against poverty and want. There are many reasons to account for this state of things of a secondary character. A good man, who regards integrity and honesty of principle as the first of all requisites in life, cannot, in his dealings with the world, stoop to mean deceptions and petty frauds, which under the name of business customs so frequently sap the foundations of commercial life. In the race for riches where there are so many reckless competitors, who disregard the sanctions of Divine morality, a Christian often falls behind, and sees dishonest and untruthful rivals rise to places of power and position. Such a man also allows his generosity oftentimes to exceed his means. He cannot hear the tale of the unfortunate without lending a helping hand, or listen to the cry of poverty without supplying its pressing wants. I know of more than one such character in our Province, who but for their generosity of soul, and liberality of purse, might have been millionaries, but still, far advanced in years, are busy toilers in the counting-room, and in the marketplace. All honour to such men, and glorious shall be their reward, when the impartial recompense of Heaven shall be awarded to an assembled universe. Rather give me the satisfaction of mind which such benevolence produces in the present world, not to speak of the noble rewards of the future, than all the gold of Peru, or the gilded palaces of princely wealth. But even supposing that the Christian is equally succesful in business with the worldling, he is not exempted from those periodical panics that shake the pillars of society, and almost instantaneously reduce men of unbounded wealth to very beggary. In these financial storms the Christian merchant often suffers most sincerely, and is left a solitary wreck, unable through life to retrieve his fortunes or recover his estates. Now, as regards the Christian, whatever be the indirect causes of his worldly misfortunes and calamities, we are to regard them as sent by his Heavenly Father for a wise end—to wean him from this world, and the treasures and refinements of this world, and lift his aspirations towards higher and purer joys. " No man can tell whether he is rich or poor by turning to his ledger. It is the heart that makes a man rich. He is rich or poor according to what *he is*, not according to what he has." Every additional dollar that is added to the store of an ungodly man, is just so much subtracted from his immortal nature; another fetter binding him to earth; another millstone dragging him down the faster to perdition. But the loss of wealth to the Christian becomes a blessing. As the ship at sea struggling with the storm and waves is lightened by throwing overboard the cargo, in order to ensure the safety of the vessel and her crew, so the loss of material good is often the salvation of the immortal soul. There is awful danger that even good men become ensnared with the riches of this world. It was a good saying of one to a great Lord, upon his showing his stately house and pleasant gardens, "Sir, you had need make sure of Heaven, or else, when you die, you will be a very great loser." But to think much about Heaven, far less to make sure of it, when a man sits among his money-bags, and is fawned upon and flattered by the crowd, is difficult to the best of men. Hence the necessity of crosses and disappointments—nay, at times of poverty itself. If the child will not gradually be weaned from the mother's breast, then it must be removed at once, whatever be the pain and sorrow that result. Better that Sodom and Gomorrah be burned up than Lot's heart become wedded to its wickedness. In order to the sure and substantial growth of a tree, it must be pruned;—in some cases cut down, in order that it may start afresh. It is not good, that it should grow too tall, or have too much foliage. There may be more leaves in that case, than blossoms or fruit. So it is not good for any man to be too successful in business. It seems as if the holiest of men needed checks—crosses—new starts in their spiritual existence to make them holier, and more prolific in good deeds. Then they can say with the apostle, "I have learned in whatever state I am, therewith to be content"—resigned to God's wise and gracious appointment, they are always happy:

"Pleased with all the Lord provides,
Weaned from all the world besides."

How strikingly different is the effect of worldly misfortunes on different men! At times, the loss of money completely overwhelms and shakes both the physical and mental constitution. Men become deranged, and are hurried to the solitariness of the mad-house. Others, not so terribly affected, go about life querulous and complaining—not overwhelmed, it may be, but overpowered; their heads turn prematurely grey, and their vital forces dry up. Others after a time become more resigned to God's appointment—they give a tacit acquiescence to God's dealings, though inwardly they feel they have been hardly smitten, and cannot see the profit of their losses. But the child of God not only submits, but feels just as happy as in his better days. He is able to rise superior to trials. He extracts from the bitterest herbs the sweetest juices, and becomes stronger for the battle of life—and more mellowed and ripened for the paradise of God, just in proportion as he is overborne and crushed under the pressure of earthly burdens. Thus he can say with David, "My soul is like a weaned child."

Third—By disappointments in earthly friendships God weans the believer from this world. This form of trial is a hard one. In this cold world how good a thing it is to have some trusty friend; one who is ever sure and sympathizing amid all the changes and conditions of existence; and yet, have we not all bitterly experienced the infidelity of those who professed the strongest attachment to our person and our interests. Perhaps we have not been so often mortified and saddened by the fickleness of earthly friendships as to say, with David, "all men are liars," but we all have felt how wise is the exhortation "put not your trust in princes, nor in the son of man, in whom there is no help." For even should your earthly attachments prove sincere —there is a time coming—just the time you need their presence and assistance most—when they pass away. "His breath goeth forth, he returneth to his earth—in that very day his thoughts perish." Now the loss of earthly friends has a powerful effect in weaning us from this world. Every newly opened grave that receives the mortal form of some true and trusty companion lessens our attachment to earth.

"There is no union here of hearts,
That finds not here an end;

But,

There surely is some blessed clime
Where life is not a breath,
Nor life's affections transient fire
Whose sparks fly upward and expire.'

When I visit on mournful errands yon graveyard, and stand for a little near the graves of many dear Christian friends now in glory, I cannot but envy them—and the thought of their ~~intermittent~~ *constant* joy, in the cloudless and tearless regions of eternity, always throws a shadow upon the vanities of the present hour. As you loved your wife, bereaved husband, and revere her memory, does not the thought of a happy reunion in Heaven serve to chasten and modify the remaining attachments of earth? It is related that after the death of Richard Cameron, the Scottish Covenanter, Peden, his life-long companion, and partner in trials, was accustomed to visit his grave upon the wild moors of Airsmoss, and longed to regain his society;—

"There came a worn and weary man to Cameron's place of rest,
He cast him down upon the sod—he smote upon his breast,
He wept as only strong men weep, when weep they must, or die,
And, 'Oh! to be wi' thee, Ritchie,' was still his bitter cry."

Fourth—God weans believers from this world *by the enlightening influences of His Spirit*, showing them the beauty and attractiveness of Christ's character and presence—the solid and lasting happiness of religion, and the good hope of the believer-beyond the grave. Chastisement and trial without Divine teaching can never make a man heavenly-minded. There must not only be the withdrawal of worldly comforts, but the supply of other and richer blessings. Much of the Christian's future good must be grasped by faith. Infinite joys can only be grasped by infinite minds, and eternal felicity by souls in their condition of pure immortality beyond the grave. But in the present life, under the operations of the Divine Spirit, there are hours when things far distant are brought near. To see God as He is, is the satisfying portion of the blessed in Heaven; but to know Him as He is may be the privilege of the faithful upon earth. As you withdraw one toy after another from the hands of childhood, you must be prepared with something else to amuse or to educate. The child cannot be weaned unless fitting nourishment is provided. So, my hearers, God provides for the advancing life of the Christian. None of them are allowed to starve. None need ever murmur like the Israelites, that there is no bread in the wilderness. The Lord not only provides glory at the end of our pilgrimage, but grace now. The Christian does not need to be an actual occupant of Heaven to enjoy many of its delights. The closing years of life are to many the land of Beulah. Here, within sight of the city, upon the borders of Canaan, they walk with Shining Ones, and refresh themselves with the dainties of the King's vineyard. Death itself is robbed of its terrors, and appears more like the fiery chariot of salvation, than the austere messenger from the grave. In George Herbert's words, "Death, thou wast once an uncouth, hideous thing; but since our Saviour's death has put some blood into thy face, thou hast grown a thing sure to be desired, and full of grace."

Brethren, are you becoming weaned from this world? One of the marks by which it may be known is humility—lowliness of mind—and contrition of spirit. There is nothing so pleasing to God as such a frame of mind, "God delights," says an old author, "to fill broken vessels and contrite spirits. Just as the silver dews flow down from the mountains to the lowest valleys, does God delight to fill the heart of the humble with the choicest blessings of his grace. The choicest buildings have the lowest foundations—those ears of corn and boughs of trees that are most filled and best laden, bow lowest,—so do the souls that are most laden with the fruits of Paradise."

The Essentials of Profitable Worship.

"Where two or three are gathered together in my name, there am I in the midst of them."—Matt. xviii. 20.

In nothing has the change which language undergoes been more strikingly exhibited than in the meaning commonly attached to the word *Church*. In its primary and proper signification, it denotes nothing more than an assembly — a gathering of people into one place, irrespective of the character of the persons congregated, or the object for which they are met. More generally under the Christian dispensation, it refers either to the whole body of Christians scattered over the world, whatever be the particular name or denomination by which they are known, or to some particular body of professing Christians. In its more limited sense it means, not simply such as have attached themselves to the visible church, but those who, in the sight of God, are worthy of a place in the invisible; the church of the first-born, whose names are written in

Heaven. But in no case, in New Testament times, is the name applied to the building where men meet for public worship. We find mention made of the Church at Jerusalem, and the Church in the House of Priscilla and Aquila, but of no special edifice, consecrated as the "Church of Christ." Living souls—earnest disciples—zealous and devoted men and women—these constituted the Church of Christ—not dead materials, but living stones in the living Temple. "To go to church" according to such a definition, was to become allied with the body of the faithful, to become one of the family of the Saints, and enjoy the fellowship of that holy brotherhood, for whom Christ died. It was not the place of meeting that bound them together, but a unity and harmony of feeling, experience, faith and hope. Whether the Church met in the upper room at Jerusalem—or upon the mountain-side—or out in the Lake of Galilee in a fishing boat—or in the gloomy dungeons of a prison, it possessed all the essentials of a Christian assembly—namely, Christ's presence to bless and comfort, for "where two or three are gathered together in His name, there He is present in their midst."

This however was new doctrine to the Jews, as indeed it may seem strange to some who now hear me. Mount Zion in Jerusalem was very dear to the pious Jew, and the temple a hallowed spot in his imagination. "Beautiful for situation, the joy of the whole earth is Mount Zion, on the sides of the north, the city of the great King—God is known in her palaces for a refuge—walk about Zion, and go round about her, tell the towers thereof. Glorious things are spoken of thee, O City of God. Thy servants take pleasure in her stones, and favour the dust thereof. The Lord hath chosen Zion; He hath desired it for His habitation." These and such like sentences, declare the fond affection entertained for the temple, and the reasons for it. It was not a groundless, unreasonable preference for Mount Zion over all other hallowed spots of Palestine. Here Solomon's great and glorious temple had been erected;—so often filled with the glory and majesty of the great King. Here, the second temple, less grand and costly, but not less precious in the eyes of the Jews, had been built after the weary years of captivity, and here, for many generations, the pious tribes repaired to give

thanks unto the name of the Lord. Even at the
present day, Mount Zion, desolate and bare—sitting
as a widow in her loneliness—is a hallowed spot to
the Christian soul, who wanders over Palestine in
the footsteps of his ascended Master. How much
more so must it be to the zealous Jew, who
daily looks for the coming of his Messiah, and the
restoration of Israel's worship, and Israel's privileges
upon Mount Zion.

At the coming of Christ, all this undue reverence
for one locality above another, as more suitable for
the worship of God, was to be done away with.
This the woman of Samaria was distinctly taught
by Christ, in His interview at Jacob's well. Just
as fondly as the Jew loved Mount Zion in Jerusalem,
did the Samaritan love Mount Gerizim in Samaria.
"Our fathers worshipped in this mountain," said
the woman of Samaria, "and ye say that in Jerusalem is the place where men ought to worship."
She could not imagine acceptable worship anywhere
else. This, in her estimation, was the only and
divinely appointed place for public worship, and indeed, as we learn from historians, "there is probably

no other locality on the face of the earth, where the same worship has sustained so little change or interruption as in this mountain, from the days of Abraham to the present. In their humble synagogue at the foot of Mount Gerizim the Samaritans still worship, the oldest and smallest sect in the world." To disabuse her mind of this erroneous and contracted idea, Christ says, "Woman, believe Me, the hour cometh, when ye shall neither in this mountain, nor yet at Jerusalem, worship the Father; the hour cometh, and now is, when the true worshippers shall worship the Father in Spirit and in truth; for the Father seeketh such to wórship Him." There is now no longer any one place especially chosen or consecrated as a place for worship; true spiritual, acceptable worship shall soon be offered everywhere—we are now approaching a period when the question will not be *where* we worship, but *what* we worship—not what are the outward circumstances of our approach to our Maker, but what are the feelings of the soul when holding intercourse with the Almighty maker of the universe. The hour is even now come when such true worshippers are worshipping the Father in spirit and in truth. "The groves," says the Poet, "were God's first Temples, and now wherever the Christian treads 'tis haunted holy ground." Communing with nature in her varied forms of beauty, God speaks to the believing soul; while under the open sky—in the forest, in the cave, and on the ocean, if the spirit of devotion be present, there is access to a prayer-hearing God.

Many Christians have not yet learned this truth. They perhaps do not idolize localities or buildings set apart for worship—nor believe that sprinkling holy water upon doors and altars or foundation stones, makes them more precious to Almighty God, or better adapted for religious worship; or that they need call in the aid of a Bishop to consecrate such buildings;—but they do have a lingering feeling that true worship must have a Church—a particular building set apart for such exercises—a place where alone it is becoming and proper to meet on the first day of the week, for the solemn duties of religion. Nor do I undervalue such a feeling, if kept within proper bounds, and held intelligently. I pity the man who has no religious home; who, like the poor outcast sitting upon the door-step, or lying out on the grassy field, instead of under the shelter of his own roof—has no preference for one Church building above another;—who has no sweet associations connected with the House of God, as the spot where first he heard the name of Jesus—where first he was baptized—where first he gave himself publicly to Christ, and heard the glad tidings of salvation. All places are not alike dear to the child of God. There are private dwellings and houses of worship which call up before the mind the holiest and happiest recollections—places "where a constant Sabbath shines, and a perpetual air of heaven reposes; where prayer has been offered and answered—where, in days of despondency and sadness, the weary spirit has been comforted and cheered by angel visits." No, if memory forgets these hallowed spots, let our right hand forget her cunning, and our tongue cleave to the roof of our mouth! We would not destroy such feelings, praiseworthy in themselves, and susceptible of the holiest joy. But we would at the same time impress upon your minds the blessed truth that wherever Christ is, there is a sanctuary. Old Isaac, in Patriarchal times, found sweet moments of contemplation in the fields—Abraham amid the groves of Beersheba—King David in glens and caverns and rocky hiding-places—the Saviour and his disciples on mountain-tops, and by the sounding sea—Paul and Silas in the dungeon at Philippi—our covenanting fathers beneath the shadow of lofty precipices, and by the margin of lonely lakes—and the Waldenses of old amid the secret clefts of Alpine fastnesses;—all found the pavilion of the Most High, where their souls were refreshed, and their hearts baptized with the dews of Heavenly grace. It does not need four walls and a bolted door, to make a place of prayer. Retirement and silence, and a devout spirit, will create it anywhere. "By the shore of the sounding sea—in the depths of the forest—in the remoteness of the green and sunny upland, or the balmy peacefulness of the garden bower—nay, amid the dust of the dingy wareroom, or the cobwebs of the owlet-haunted barn; in the jutting corner of the crowded stage, or the unnoticed nook of the traveller's room, you have only to shut your eyes and seclude your spirit, and you have a place where the soul may find itself alone with God."

This, I apprehend, is the teaching of Christ in our text. What, then, are the essentials of profitable worship—of sincere, heartfelt communion with God? Not numbers—not the place of meeting;—but, first, the spirit of devotion; and, secondly, the presence of Christ, which is always found where the spirit of devotion exists.

First—Not numbers. Two or three constitute a Church, and the most influential Churches in our land have had such beginnings. How small the early Christian apostolic Church in Jerusalem! Eleven humble disciples, and a few pious women, and yet Christ rejoiced to come into their assembly and give them His benediction. And from that little band there went out the pioneers of the world's conversion, whose successors now, in every region of the globe, unfurl the banner of the Cross, and raise the standard of Truth. I know well that there is an enthusiasm in numbers. I know that, other things being equal, a large influential, and wealthy membership, can more efficiently operate upon society than a feeble, struggling enterprize. But while this is true, numbers have their serious drawbacks, as well as their advantages. The spirit of Christian love too often cools, instead of expands; liberality too often ebbs; active efforts for the conversion of souls, on the part of the individual is relaxed; attendance upon ordinances is more irregular, and the spirit of earnest prayer restrained. Neither worldly nor spiritual prosperity is in proportion to numbers. The spirit must move the wheels, and love to God and men's souls fire the heart, otherwise large congregations become like the valley of visions, full of bones—very many, and very dry.

Now, while the truth here announced is full of comfort to ministers and devoted Christians, who lament the few who come up to Zion's solemnities —the scarcity of attendance on prayer-meetings, and the irregular attendance of professing church members upon ordinances—it affords no grounds for absence to such as systematically and without excuse turn their backs upon the sanctuary. It is very true God will not allow His people to suffer through your neglect; however much the minister may be disheartened, and His people discouraged by your inconsistent conduct, the Word, if preached in faith, will profit, and God's presence will be manifest. But the "two or three" who meet together from week to week, for prayer and fellowship, might be stimulated and cheered by your presence to greater achievements in the Church of Christ. There is a spiritual magnetism, and sympathy of soul which numbers impart. When Zion's gates are crowded; when the number of the saints are increased; when the song of praise ascending to the throne on high is like the sound of many waters, and the accustomed place of meeting becomes too strait for the throng of worshippers, then may we expect the dawn of that glorious period when Christians shall be born in a day, and the dark places of the earth illumined with the Sun of Righteousness.

Second.—Not the place of meeting. God can hear and answer prayer anywhere. The scaffold—the fiery furnace—the dungeon—the condemned cell—the drowning waters, have all at various times, in the history of the Church, become hallowed with the praises and the triumphant testimonies of martyrs. The merchant may have a church in his counting-house—

and the manufacturer in his factory. On the corners of the streets, and upon the house-top, Christ and Him crucified may be preached with vast effect. The theatre, the dance-room, the bar-room, the senate chamber, and the court-room, have all at times, in these recent years of awakening, become Bethels—places where ladders have been uplifted between heaven and earth, and where God's angels have ascended and descended, carrying the glad news of converted sinners. But for the steady, decorous, and stated exercises of a church, a building is necessary—a place where God's saints may take refuge from the cares of life, and where, undisturbed and undistracted by the bustle of the world, they may meditate upon things unseen and eternal. Such a place we occupy to-day, and consecrate for the time being to Almighty God.* Thankful should we be that, while God has put it into our hearts to beautify and adorn our "Zion," we have such a sanctuary, where, in comfort and in safety, we can meet together;—where, without fear of man, or the threat of persecution, a full and free gospel can

---

* While worshipping in the "Music Hall."

be offered, and where, as in bygone years, we may hope to gather in wanderers to the fold of Christ. While for a little we tarry together in our tabernacle, let us pray for the outpouring of God's spirit to fill this building with His glory—to make it illustrious for the salutary impressions that shall be made by the preaching of the gospel, so that in the day of God it may be said of many blood-bought saints, "This and that man was born here."

Let us now look at the essentials of profitable worship. *First—The spirit of Devotion*—a frame of mind in keeping with the House of God—in harmony with the exercises to be engaged in, and expectant of blessings. The Israelites were commanded to sanctify themselves ere they ventured into the presence of God. Moses was commanded to take his shoes from off his feet, when he stood near the burning bush, for the place was holy ground; and so should we in drawing near into the immediate presence of Jehovah. "God is greatly to be feared in the assembly of His saints, and to be had in reverence of all them that are about Him." Nothing can better fit a man for the service of the sanctuary, than a realizing sense of his personal unworthiness—his depravity and pollution, and the wondrous condescending grace that nevertheless accepts such a sinner. This is the first requisite in order to communion with God. It matters not whether, like the Pharisee of old, we occupy the chief seat in the temple, or the lowest, provided we have the feelings of the publican, which led him to cry out, "God, be merciful to me, a sinner."

I feel, brethren, that while I insist upon a devotional spirit as the essential requisite for the enjoyment of ordinances, it is one of those experiences or graces that can scarcely be described in so many words. And yet, who does not know what we mean when we say, "Such a man is very devoted to his business!" We mean that there is an entire and unconditional surrender of the heart with its powers, affections, and emotions to a certain object—a concentration of mind for a certain purpose and a special end. Devotion, then, applied to Christian worshippers, implies a yielding of the heart to the Supreme Being, with that reverence

—that faith and joy, that is becoming a redeemed and ransomed soul. It is the solemn consciousness, that we stand unclothed in the presence of the Omniscient—that our thoughts, purposes, and acts of worship are all scanned and scrutinized by Him whose eyes are as a flaming fire. It is just what John felt, when about to gaze in apocalyptic vision upon the Son of man as he walked among the golden candlesticks, where, he tells us, "I was in the Spirit on the Lord's day," and when under the awful splendour of His glory "*he fell at His feet as dead.*" It is the swallowing up of the creature in the Creator—the emptying oneself of everything that is secular and secularizing, that God Himself may come into the soul, and claim its undivided allegiance and love.

Do we not all lack the devotional spirit in the House of God which should characterize sincere worshippers? The King is prepared to meet the guests, but we are not prepared to see the King. The table is spread, but we have not the relish for the banquet. The fountain is flowing, but we do not thirst for its waters. I do not depreciate secret, silent prayer in the sanctuary;—it is doubtless valuable in calming the distracted soul, and preparing for the song of praise; but, after all, the preparation best suited for the devotion of the sanctuary must be made at home and in the closet. It is there that wrestling and struggling for the minister—for the office-bearers of the Church —for the success of the Sabbath-School—for your own individual profit and enjoyment under the preaching of the Gospel, must begin, and, when earnestly engaged in, it never fails.

Do not confound a devotional spirit with a gloomy, sepulchral, terror-stricken and slavish state of mind, that comes trembling to the throne of grace. You no longer stand at the base of Mount Sinai—that Mount that burned with fire, and over whose summit storm and tempest raged, "but ye are come unto Mount Zion, and unto the City of the Living God. * * * To Jesus, the mediator of the new covenant, and to the blood of sprinkling, that speaketh better things than the blood of Abel." Perfect love casteth out fear; and such love all God's children should possess.

"Boldly," though not with presumptuous confidence, are we to come into God's presence—assured of our acceptance and welcome—just as the affectionate child comes bounding into the presence of a loving father, without the faintest thought of a repulse. The Scriptures clearly teach us that there may be gravity and sobriety of conduct united to heartfelt joy and gladness. We are to come into His presence with thanksgiving—making a joyful noise unto Him with psalms. While we worship in the beauty of holiness, we are at the same time to call upon the heavens to rejoice, and the earth to be glad, because of the marvellous things which the Lord hath done. On the day of the resurrection, when the disciples, downcast and sad in spirit, were assembled in Jerusalem, Jesus unexpectedly came into their midst, saying unto them, "Peace be unto you," and instantly their feelings were changed from gloom to cheerfulness. "Then were the disciples glad when they saw the Lord." And though no longer present in the flesh, and visible to the eye of sense, Christ can as certainly be apprehended and seen by the eye of Faith in the sanctuary. Surely such a sight should make glad the hearts of God's people at all times. The fact of the resurrection, which the return of the weekly Sabbath so directly commemorates, is surely to us, as it was to them, a ground of thankfulness and praise. It is not befitting that we should keep our happiest frames of mind, and most cheerful expressions of countenance, for the social and less sacred gatherings of the week. When the bride comes into the presence of the bridegroom, her face is radiant with smiles; and when God's people come up to Mount Zion their hearts should glow with sacred fire, and their tongues exult in rapturous melody. Our language to companion saints should be,

"Come we that love the Lord,
And let our joys be known,
Join in a song with sweet accord,
And thus surround the throne.

" The hill of Zion yields,
A thousand sacred sweets,
Before we reach the Heavenly fields,
Or walk the golden streets.

"Then let our songs abound,
And every tear be dry,
We're marching through Immanuel's ground
To fairer worlds on high."

But the other essential of acceptable worship is *the presence of Christ*. The presence of Christ may be understood in various senses. As the Omniscient God, He is everywhere to be found, throughout the regions of immensity. As a sympathizing friend, He is ever near the afflicted believer, and is thoroughly acquainted with all his wants. He is also with the Church in her varied trials and sufferings. The Son of man is still in the burning bush—and therefore the Psalmist sings, "God is in the midst of her; she shall not be moved; God shall help her, and that right early." The promise made to Zechariah has never once failed;—"I will be unto her a wall of fire and the glory in the midst of her." But the promise of Christ's presence in the text especially refers, I imagine, to the stated ordinances of the sanctuary. The context shows this. He is *here* with his worshipping people, in a very different sense than He is present in other assemblies. "Lo! I am with you alway, even unto the end of the world." All the days—without withdrawal or intermission—unto perpetuity—such was His promise to the disciples when giving them their commission to go forth and preach the Gospel. And to the same purport are the words of our text. When engaged in His service, as pastor and people, we are certain of Christ's aid and blessing. As Matthew Henry says, "There is no day, nor hour of the day, in which our Lord Jesus is not present with His churches and His ministers; if there were, that day, that hour, they were undone. The God of Israel, the Saviour, is sometimes a God that hideth Himself, but never a God that absenteth Himself; sometimes in the dark—never at a distance." Wherever or whenever two or three are gathered together—it matters not what the particular denomination—whether the Church assembled pride themselves on being the real descendants of the Apostolic Church, or glory in their non-conformity;—if there is a sincere desire to commune with Heaven, there He is present—present as a Spirit of grace, revealing Christ and God's truth to the heart and conscience; present in the sacraments—present with the minister as a spirit of enlightenment, and present with the people as the indwelling hope of glory. Now what does this presence of Christ secure to His Church? *It secures the Divine authority and approval of all its acts and exercises*, whether of dis-

cipline or of worship, when these are observed in
accordance with His revealed will. We do not
meet under the shelter of royalty, nor derive our
rights and liberties from any secular power. We
hold it to be the duty of the civil power to aid
the Church in so far as preventing any interference
with the rights of conscience; but our authority, as
a Church, is spiritual, and depends not on the whims
and sufferances of peers and judges. Jesus Christ
by the promise of His presence in the assemblies
of His people, asserts His Kingly Headship over
the Church, and any Church that surrenders its
laws and spiritual acts to the judgment of the civil
power is false to its Divine origin. We cannot too
often at the present day assert this truth, when
certain Churches, at the bidding of civil authority,
basely yield their Heaven - derived prerogatives
rather than cast themselves upon the free-will offerings of the people, and the provision of the Master.
But, in addition, Christ's presence in the Church
secures continued success to the preaching of the Gospel.
The minister in undertaking his life labour at the
call of Heaven can confidently cast himself upon
a higher power than his own unaided reason. His

highest qualifications come driect from Heaven, and these are never withheld from sincere and faithful preachers. All the efficiency of the pulpit—the successive seasons of revival that from age to age have increased the Church, the spread of truth beyond Christian lands, and the gradual decay of heathenism and error—is due not to the *letter*, but to the *spirit*; not to the agency, but to the quickening power of Almighty God. And just in proportion as we rely upon God's blessing in all our stated appeals from Sabbath to Sabbath, will we the more fully realize Christ's presence. In proportion to the vivid consciousness of our wants, will be the rich and satisfying displays of wondrous grace in the sanctuary.

The continued existence of the Church to the present day is the most striking of all testimonies that the Divine presence is with her. It is not in her own resources that she has accomplished the mighty reforms in morals and religion which the history of our race in the past discloses. It is not by her own inherent energy or vitality that she now lives, and continues her aggressive efforts against superior forces. Her ordinances are simple —her creed is pervaded by no persecuting spirit— her movements are silent and hidden compared to great and mighty enterprises that startle and shake society. But yet she conquers, and has never known real defeat. Why? Because her existence is eternal, prolonged by the infinite power and will of Heaven, whose appointed instrument she is for the redemption of a fallen world.

Brethren, do you desire Christ's presence in the services of the Church? Then you must possess the spirit which the promise demands. There is a condition attached. Not in every congregation is the Maker present—only in such as are assembled in *His name.* Our prayer must be, in coming to the sanctuary, that God's glory may be more increasingly manifested before the world in the conversion of souls. Our aim must be Christ's aim —our will His will. If any other motive or purpose brings you to the House of God—mere curiosity—or custom—or worldly policy—or the maintaining of a Christian character bofore the world—or the passing of an hour or two that lies heavy on your hands, because labour is suspended, and the wheels of commerce are at rest;—or a desire to see and be seen—or to have the taste gratified by the charms of music or oratory;—then you cannot expect God's presence or His accompanying blessing. I do not say you shall reap no good whatever—for separation from the haunts of evil and vice is a negative advantage of vast importance. Nor do I say that you commit a sin in thus acting which is unpardonable, but what I say is, that, failing to come up to the requirements of the text, you cannot offer spiritual and acceptable worship. When Christ comes to meet His people in His house, they must come prepared to meet Him in His own appointed way.

These remarks are of course more directly applicable to God's own children. It is a comforting thought that, in the ordinances of the Church, a Saviour is often found by those who seek Him not; that some who come to scoff remain to pray, and some who come to laugh are made to weep. Many sceptics, under the faithful, earnest presentation of the truth, have been forced to cry out like the doubting Thomas, "My Lord and my God." One of the greatest, if not the very greatest, of English living preachers at the present day, traces his conversion to what we would call the accidental hearing of a sermon. In the first of his published volumes he thus writes; " Six years ago to-day, as near as possible at this very hour of the day, I was in the gall of bitterness and in the bonds of iniquity, but had yet, by Divine grace, been led to feel the bitterness of that bondage, and to cry out by reason of the soreness of the slavery. Seeking rest, and finding none, I stepped into the House of God and sat there, afraid to look upward lest I should be utterly cut off, and lest His fierce wrath should consume me. The minister rose in his pulpit, and, as I have done this morning, read this text, 'Look unto me, and be ye saved, all the ends of the earth, for I am God, and there is none else.' I looked that moment; and the grace of faith was vouchsafed to me in the selfsame instant, and now I think I can say with truth—

> "' E'er since by faith I saw the stream,
> His flowing wounds supply,
> Redeeming love has been my theme,
> And shall be till I die.' "

"I shall never," says Spurgeon, "forget that day while memory holds its place." And who knows, my hearers, but within these walls the power of God's truth may be as effectually witnessed in the conversion of not one but many souls. Be it so, Oh, Thou Spirit of all Good, and to Thy name, throughout all eternity, shall be the praise.

www.ingramcontent.com/pod-product-compliance
Lightning Source LLC
Chambersburg PA
CBHW030407230426
43664CB00007BB/783